LOST TREASURES
of the World

LOST TREASURES
of the World

Michael Groushko

CHARTWELL
BOOKS, INC.

This book was devised and produced by
Multimedia Publications (UK) Ltd

Editor: Richard Rosenfeld
Assistant editors: Edward Bunting,
Tony Hall, Dan Millar
Research: Arthur Butterfield, Ian Knight
Production: Karen Bromley
Design: Richard Carr John Strange Associates
Picture Research: Anne Horton

Published by
CHARTWELL BOOKS, INC.
A Division of **BOOK SALES, INC.**
110 Enterprise Avenue
Secaucus, New Jersey 07094

ISBN 1 55521 044 9

Typeset by Letterspace Limited
Origination by Imago
Printed in Italy by Sagdos, Milan

Endpapers:
The destruction of the Spanish
Armada in 1588. Many Spanish
ships surviving the battle were later
wrecked off the British west coast,
which is an excellent hunting
ground for treasure-seekers.

Page 1:
A diver retrieves an ancient
amphora (wine-jar) from the floor
of the Mediterranean off the coast
of Turkey. The continuing
revolution in underwater
technology is constantly opening
up new areas of exploration to
archaeologists and treasure-
seekers.

Pages 2–3:
The Step Pyramid at Saqqara in
Egypt was the tomb of King Zoser
and his chief minister Im-Hotep.
Such pyramids have yielded the
kind of riches every treasure-hunter
dreams about.

Page 5:
A devil guarding the entrance to the
church at Rennes le Château in
Southern France. In the 1890s the
village priest found a treasure
hoard in the churchyard: reputedly
part of it is still hidden there.

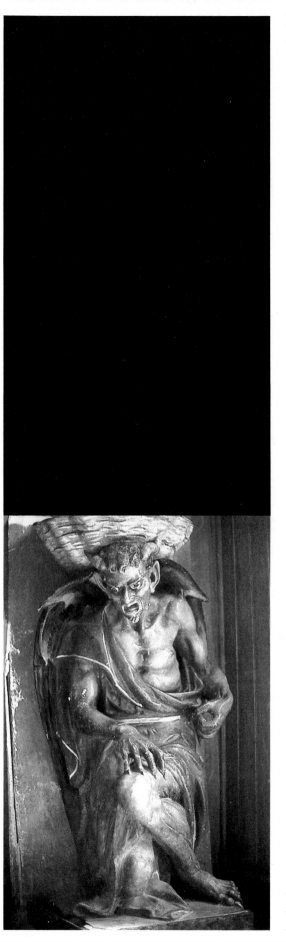

Introduction

'When I first saw it I knew what it was – a reef of silver bars. I just started screaming... I kind of lost control of myself.'

The speaker was young diver Andy Matrochi, one of the team that found perhaps the most exciting lost treasure located in our time, a laden Spanish galleon that sank off the coast of Florida more than 360 years ago and is now yielding gold, silver, and gems worth $450 million. The wreck was 16 years of dedication and danger in the finding, and every treasure-hunter's dream come true.

But for every secret hoard the earth gives up, there is another still to be traced, from the reputed treasures of the ancient conquerors to the latterday spoils of Adolf Hitler. Clues as to their whereabouts lie in misty legends and in modern bank vaults, for those with perseverance enough to track them down.

Famous examples of treasures lost and found are detailed in the following pages; who knows, their dramatic stories may even inspire you to begin treasure-hunting in a small way yourself. Remember, the past is all around us, its secrets ready to be discovered by whoever looks the hardest, and that does not just mean the professional treasure-seeker with his impressive array of resources.

The advent of high technology has turned treasure-hunting into big business, but without stripping it of any of its romantic appeal. For the technology can be used only when the approximate site has been located.

One aspect of treasure-hunting that is changing, however, is its relationship with branches of academic study, particularly archaeology and history. No longer is it respectable, if it ever was, to strip potential sites with explosives to secure their treasure while destroying intrinsically valueless but archaeologically invaluable material. Governments are placing increasing restrictions on the granting of exploration licenses, and archaeologists and other specialists are now members of many exploration teams.

It is no part of this book's purpose to encourage the plundering of archaeological sites or the invasion of private property. *Appendix II* describes the law as it applies in general to treasure-hunting (or, for that matter, archaeological investigation), with some further guidelines to good conduct. To those should be added one more: context – the surroundings and circumstances in which objects are found, and the spatial relationships between those objects – is all-important in modern archaeology. Expert advice should always be sought *before* disturbing a site.

To armchair and active treasure-hunters, the quest holds many thrills independent of the actual find. It is only at the last stage that technology and academic expertise need come into play. Until that moment, any treasure-hunter can be as alone with the secret dream as he or she wishes. Good hunting!

Far right:
This 16th-century map of South America shows in considerable, if inaccurate, detail the sources of Spain's wealth in the New World. The most obvious omission is the mountain chain of the Andes running down the western coast, the backbone of the kingdom of the fabulously rich Incas. Plunder from their territories supplied much of the cargo of the first Spanish treasure fleets.

Chapter 1

X Marks the Spot

Top right:
Edward Teach (died 1718), nicknamed Blackbeard, established a fearsome reputation in just two or three years of piracy off the Atlantic coast of what is now the USA. He heightened his frightening appearance by attaching lighted tapers to his beard when going into the fray. His courage and cruelty became legendary. Blackbeard was also a latterday Bluebeard, marrying and murdering upwards of a dozen wives. They were said to have been incarcerated in a secret, and untraced, vault where Teach stored his spoils.

The chances of tracing pirate hauls, or any other form of hidden wealth, except by accident, recede the further one goes back in history. If records exist at all, they have usually become distorted over the years, or embellished by repetition to the point where any factual basis has disappeared under layers of myth. So would-be seekers of pirate gold must turn to more recent events, where there is at least some possibility of sifting fact from fiction. Effectively, that denotes a period from the Middle Ages onwards.

Modern piracy is generally held to have had its beginnings in the 13th century. Most of the pirates of the age retained at least nominal fealty to their rulers – among them the French corsairs who operated from the Channel ports from Dunkirk to St Malo, and from Nantes and La Rochelle in the Bay of Biscay. They were privately financed by local merchants, and at first their victims were English trade ships. Later, they extended their depredations to vessels of any maritime power with which France was in dispute, and eventually they were granted official status as licensed privateers whose activities were approved by the French Minister of the Navy. (The system of privateering, in which individual captains were given free rein to harass enemy shipping and ports, lasted into the 19th century.)

In most cases, the corsairs handed over their booty to their backers, retaining only a small portion for themselves and their crews as a sort of fee for their work. But occasionally greed got the better of them, and they concealed part of the haul, intending to reclaim it later. There are several legends of corsair prizes hidden along the French channel coast.

The rise of deep-sea piracy
On his first trip to the Americas, Columbus acquired gold nuggets from Hispaniola. When he displayed them at the court of King Ferdinand and Queen Isabella of Spain, he unleashed a bout of gold fever such as the world had never seen. The Portuguese had already discovered a new source of the precious metal at Elmina in the Gold Coast (now Ghana), and the Spaniards had no wish to be left behind. By the mid-1500s, the stage was set for full-blooded ransacking of the new territories. Gold, silver, jewels, and precious artifacts were being sent by the boatload back to Spain, offering prizes that no official enemy or independent pirate could resist. Since that time they have provided a constant thread in the annals of

treasure-hunting, exerting a lure as powerful now as it was two or three centuries ago. The newfound wealth of Spain and, to a lesser extent, Portugal, attracted the envious eyes of many from the start. The corsairs of France were the first into the fray; in 1522, Jean d'Ango of Dieppe captured Spanish caravels carrying 45,000 gold pesos from Mexico, in a battle off the Azores. Soon men like François le Clerc, nicknamed 'Wooden Leg', and Jacques de Sores were raiding Spanish bases in the West Indies. De Sores held Havana for nearly three weeks in 1555, cramming his ships with gold and silver, slaughtering the inhabitants and burning the settlement to the ground.

Sir Francis Drake

Prominent among English seafarers of the same period was Francis Drake, who raided settlements up and down the Panama coast, including the port of Nombre de Dios, nicknamed 'the world's treasure-store', and captured more than 100 Spanish vessels. His most glittering prize was the treasure-ship *Nuestra Señora de la Concepción* in the Pacific off Ecuador, carrying 13 chests of coins, 80 pounds (in weight) of gold bars, and 26 tons of silver. That exploit earned Drake a knighthood from Queen Elizabeth I and made him one of the richest men in England. His exploits inspired generations of pirates on the Spanish Main, and provided early authenticated examples of two traditional ingredients of any quest for pirate treasure − secret charts and a buried cache.

The charts came from *Nuestra Señora de la Concepción* and showed the route used by Spanish galleons sailing laden with silks and spices from the Philippines to Mexico. They provide valuable clues for modern-day treasure-seekers. The treasure-cache was somewhere on the Caribbean side of the Isthmus of Panama, near the Royal Road along which the Spaniards brought gold and silver for transshipment across the Atlantic.

Barbary corsairs harry Spain

From the early 1500s, before their treasure-fleets were menaced by their north European rivals, the Spaniards faced a maritime threat much nearer home. It came from the feared Barbary corsairs, Muslim pirates operating from bases on the North African coast and owing loose allegiance to the rulers of Turkey.

Left:
Jean (or John) Lafitte, who died in 1854, is probably the best-known US pirate, not only for his exploits as buccaneer, smuggler and slave-trader, but also for his part in defeating the British at the Battle of New Orleans in 1815. Tales of his deeds, and of his undiscovered treasure caches, are part of the folklore of the bayou country of Louisiana.

Above:
Hernán Cortés (1485-1547) led a force of 600 Spanish conquistadores in subjugating Mexico from 1519 onward – an invasion that laid the basis for Spain's power and wealth in the Americas, and for three centuries of treasure shipments from the New World to the Old. In the 16th-century painting above, the Spanish conquistadores are shown on horseback; they introduced the horse to America.

Far right:
Montezuma II (right) was ruler of the Aztec empire from 1502 to 1520. His gold-rich kingdom attracted the attentions of the Spanish then establishing themselves in the New World, and Montezuma was captured by Hernán Cortés (left) in 1519. The Aztec was first held hostage in his capital of Tenochtitlán (Mexico City), and later killed by his own subjects when he was persuaded by Cortés to try and quell an uprising against the Spanish.

The Spaniards were the corsairs' main target, but they regarded all Christian nations with the same contemptuous hatred, plundering the French and the Venetians with almost equal fervor. In the 16th century, Algiers was the corsairs' headquarters; one of their number, Arouj, known as Barbarossa from his red beard, at one stage became ruler of the city by the simple expedient of murdering the Emir. His cruelty was such that the Spaniards and the Algerians joined forces against him. Barbarossa fled into the desert scattering treasure behind him to try to distract his pursuers, but they caught and killed him. Command of the corsairs went to his brother, Kheyr-ed-Din, who shared the family red hair and his brother's nickname, but was a much shrewder leader. He strengthened the ties with Turkey, led corsair raids on the Spanish vessels en route from the New World in the Atlantic, and drove Spain out of North Africa.

European pirates in the Mediterranean
In the latter years of England's war against Spain in the 16th century, English ships had begun to appear in the Mediterranean, ostensibly to harry the Spaniards there, but they were not above raiding vessels of other nations if these offered rich pickings. Soon dozens of English seamen were cruising the Mediterranean, proving the truth of a comment by the contemporary French historian Joseph Scaliger: 'None make better pirates than the English.'

In 1604, England's peace treaty with Spain and James I's disapproval of privateering made these freebooters pirates in English law as well as in Spanish name. They needed a local base, and found it in Tunis, where the Turkish ruler gave them refuge in return for the right to buy their plunder at very favorable prices.

Algiers, the old headquarters of the Barbary corsairs, was not so welcoming as Tunis to European renegades. In 1609, the acting English consul, Richard Allen, seized three Turkish vessels carrying cargo valued at 300,000 pieces-of-eight and fled with them to Spain. A year later, a Flemish freebooter called Simon Danser went one better, seizing 400,000 crowns and four ships in which he headed for Marseilles, slaughtering 150 Turks in the process.

By 1621, when the English navy blockaded Algiers, there were few Europeans left there. The same was true of Tunis. In their heyday, between 1592 and 1609, the Mediterranean corsairs had captured an average of 140 to 160 vessels a year.

Into the Atlantic

The peace of 1604, between England and Spain after nearly 20 years of constant warfare at sea, left England with a large, and now superfluous, reserve of battle-hardened sailors, most of whom were unfitted or disinclined to seek their livelihoods ashore. It was natural and inevitable that many should turn their experience to good account on their own behalf, as pirates. Once the decision was taken, there was little chance of going back, in the strict climate of James I's reign.

Some looked to the Mediterranean and the Barbary Coast for spoils and havens. But to many, the Atlantic offered more attractive opportunities. During the years of war, some licensed privateers who had strayed over the line into piracy, or gone 'on the account' in the slang of the day, were able to use English coves or harbors as bases, notably in Devon and Cornwall, remote from the authorities in London. But after 1604 that became extremely risky if not impossible, and the Atlantic pirates looked elsewhere. Two areas particularly commended themselves – Morocco and the west coast of Ireland. Thanks to Henry Mainwaring, an Oxford scholar who briefly turned pirate and then wrote a book on piracy, we have the earliest detailed picture of how the sea-raiders operated. More important for the treasure-seeker, his work, called *Of the Beginnings, Practices and Suppression of Pirates,* lists in detail the pirates' main ports of call in the early 17th century – an excellent starting-point for a search for relics.

In Morocco, the pirates made their headquarters at Mamora, near the Moorish pirate citadel of Sallee. But Mamora was not a satisfactory base for long. Both the Spaniards and the Dutch managed to blockade it – the Spaniards in 1611 sank ships across the harbor entrance, and in 1614 a Spanish fleet finally captured the town.

The rugged coast of Ireland, with its countless inlets and a population both remote from the authorities in London and Dublin and contemptuous of them, was a far better bet. Most of the pirates made their headquarters around Roaringwater Bay, in the extreme southwest, with Leamcon as their main base. Pirate colonies also grew up on Long Island and Sherkin Island and, farther north, on Whiddy Island in Bantry Bay.

The golden age

In 1628, a Dutch fleet under the command of Admiral Pieter Hein succeeded in waylaying a convoy of Spanish treasure-ships off the coast of Cuba, forcing them into Matanzas Bay, where they were wrecked on sandbanks. Reports of the number of Spanish vessels vary, but there could have been as many as 24. In any case, the Dutch had to refloat four of them to help carry the vast booty home, as all 28 Dutch ships were laden to the gunwales with treasure. Even so, they did not take all of it, and some is reputed still to lie on the bed of the bay.

The exploit helped to inspire the growing bands of European corsairs, criminals and deserters flocking to the Spanish Main in search of their fortunes. They made their base on Tortuga, a small forested island now known as Tortue just off the north coast of Haiti. It eventually grew into an important haven for pirates, and even now has not yielded up all its secrets.

Renegades from the Low Countries soon joined the French, among them Alexander Exquemelin, whose book *De Americaensche Zee-Roovers* (Buccaneers of the Americas) is almost as useful to modern-day treasure-seekers as Mainwaring's work of 60 years earlier, and Roche Brasiliano, who specialized in lightning assaults on Spanish settlements such as Campeche in Mexico. Together, they ushered in what has been called 'the golden age of piracy'.

English pirates, driven from their eastern Atlantic hunting-grounds by improved naval patrols, also came to the Caribbean in growing numbers. Some found refuge at Tortuga and Le Petit Goave, off the west coast of Haiti. However, Port Royal in Jamaica was far more welcoming. From there, Henry Morgan sailed on his raids to Maracaibo in Venezuela – like Campeche, one of the pirates' favorite targets – and the stronghold of Panama City. Port Royal's role as a pirate base lasted until 1692, when an earthquake tipped half of the town into the sea. The submerged site is a favorite hunting-ground for treasure-seekers.

The pirates go east

Now that Port Royal was no longer available to them, the pirates began to look for more suitable havens. One group, led by the Englishman John Avery and the American Henry Tew, shifted its sphere of operations to the Red Sea and the Indian Ocean, based on Madagascar, where St Mary's Island (Ile Ste Marie) gained almost as much notoriety as Port Royal had once enjoyed. It was to St Mary's Island that William Kidd sailed in 1698 after apparently turning from pirate-hunter to pirate. At the southern tip of Madagascar, at Ranter Bay, another collection of pirates installed themselves under a self-styled 'king', the Jamaican-born James Plantain.

Northeast of Madagascar, the islands of the Seychelles were another favorite pirate haven. In the 1720s, the notorious Frenchman Olivier Lavasseur, nicknamed 'The Buzzard', based himself there to prey on shipping, and one of his prizes was a vessel carrying $140 million in treasure belonging to the Bishop of Goa, the

Left:
The great medieval trading organization known as the Hanseatic League, with its bases in all the main European ports around the Baltic and North Sea, was one of the earliest targets for organized piracy. A gang of seaborne raiders, who called themselves 'Friends of God and Enemies of the World', preyed on Hanseatic shipping. In 1402, one of the pirate leaders, Stertebeker (or Stoertebeck), and 70 of his accomplices were captured and executed at Hamburg, in what is now Germany. This 16th-century picture shows the pirates lined up for the executioner's sword.

Far left:
A hero to the English, a pirate to the Spanish, Sir Francis Drake (?1540-96) commanded a marauding fleet off Spanish America from 1585. He captured more than 100 Spanish vessels, including the treasure-laden *Nuestra Señora de la Concepción*, and his exploits fired the imaginations of many during the golden age of piracy.

Portuguese colony in India. Lavasseur was eventually caught and hanged; as he went to the gallows he threw a paper to the crowd, bearing a cryptic message indicating where the Goan treasure was hidden.

Years later, it came into the hands of a former East African big-game hunter called Reginald Wilkins. He narrowed the location of the site down to Belle Ombre Bay on the island of Mahi, an area of underground caves and tunnels. Wilkins believed he was within six yards of the cache when he died in 1977. Since then, the site has been neglected and become overgrown. Recent surveys revealed a metal object the size of a dining-table in the sand of the bay, and plans to investigate it further were being prepared early in 1986.

Back to the Americas

For a while, Nassau in the Bahamas provided a refuge for pirates, at least for those who could bribe the governor. Avery was attempting to do just that when his ship, the *Fancy,* foundered on a reef outside the harbor, carrying at least some treasure to the value of $420,000. It has never been traced. Nassau had earlier been a base for the fearsome Edward Teach, known as 'Blackbeard', who terrorized merchantmen in the waters from Virginia to Florida between 1716 and 1718. It is said that he kept his treasure in a secret underground vault, where he also periodically walled up a succession of his wives.

By the early 1800s, the golden age of piracy was drawing to a close; almost its final flourish was provided by America's most notorious pirates, the brothers Jean and Pierre Lafitte. They operated from Barataria Bay on the coast of Louisiana, an inlet entered from a narrow channel between the islands of Grande Terre and Grande Ile, which the Lafittes fortified with cannon.

In 1814, the British navy tried in vain to enlist the Lafittes' support in the war against the United States. Eventually the Americans enlisted the pirates' help in defeating the British in the Battle of New Orleans. In return, they received a letter of thanks and free pardons –

Right:
Christopher Columbus (1451-1506) made his first landfall in the New World on 12th October 1492, on the Bahamian island of San Salvador, or Watling Island; the event is shown here in a romanticized 19th-century print. Columbus's boastful tales of his achievement won him few friends at the court of his sponsors, King Ferdinand and Queen Isabella of Spain. But the gold nuggets he brought back with him convinced the Spanish that he had found a source of hitherto undreamed-of wealth, and unleashed a murderous treasure hunt that has no parallel in history.

not nearly enough, in Jean Lafitte's view. He went back to piracy, operating from an island off the coast of Texas. That base was destroyed by the US navy in 1821, but Jean Lafitte escaped to re-emerge later under a false name in the guise of a respectable merchant, a role he successfully maintained until his death in 1854.

Tales are still told in the bayous of Louisiana of hidden caches made by the Lafitte brothers, although the evidence suggests that most of the treasure they accumulated was either disposed of or seized by the authorities. One thing is certain, however; in their lifetimes, old-style piracy virtually vanished.

A seeker's guide
For treasure-seekers looking for likely hiding-places – the islands of the Caribbean and the American Atlantic seaboard, the west coast of Ireland, Madagascar, and the islands of the Indian Ocean, for example – several points are worth bearing in mind. First, both pirates and their victims generally played down the values of their hauls.

Second, there was little incentive for out-and-out rogues from the 17th century onwards to bury their treasure. Exceptions might arise if a haul was too great to be carried off in the available vessels, or if returning pirates got wind of an imminent raid on their base. Searches around such bases could yield a huge cache – but are more likely to reveal small (though valuable) quantities of items overlooked or lost.

The group with the biggest incentive to conceal treasure in remote places were privateers who went to the bad – a category that may embrace the likes of Kidd and Morgan. Even if the crews did not know the precise hiding-place (and care was generally taken to ensure they did not), they must have known the rough location, from where the ship put in and a few people went ashore. Back at base, and in their cups, some must have dropped heavy hints to anyone who would listen.

That is why tales of Morgan's treasure, spoken of by his crew though not by him, ring more true than those of Kidd, attested only by himself – and why a study of the privateers may ultimately be more rewarding than a pursuit of the likes of Blackbeard.

The quest for Kidd's cache

CAPTAIN KYDD CONCEALING TREASURE IN A CAVERN.

When Captain William Kidd was hanged for piracy at London's Execution Dock on 23rd May 1701, he can hardly have foreseen the legacy he was leaving to future generations. For Kidd, more than any one person, has provided the basis for the stereotype pirate, possessor of the secret of a hidden treasure hoard. The stereotype has been embellished by a succession of writers of fiction who drew upon Kidd's exploits as source material – among them James Fenimore Cooper, Edgar Allan Poe and, above all, Robert Louis Stevenson in *Treasure Island.*

Stevenson's classic novel contains all the ingredients we have come to expect in a pirate yarn – a cryptic map, a mysterious island, buried gold, mayhem, murder and the thrill of the quest. Some of these ingredients occurred in the lives of real pirates, but Kidd's history contains *every* one, in full measure.

Kidd's place both in romantic fiction and in the annals of treasure-hunting was secured by a dramatic act on the eve of his execution. In a desperate attempt to save himself from the gallows, he wrote to the Speaker of England's House of Commons promising to reveal the whereabouts of some of his accumulated spoils in return for his life.

Said Kidd: 'In my proceedings in the Indies, I have lodged goods and Tresure to the value of £100,000, which I desiere the Government may have the benefit of, in order thereto I shall desiere no manner of liberty, but to be kept prisoner on board such ship as may be appointed for that purpose and only give the necessary directions. And in case I faile therein, I shall desiere no favour but to be forthwith executed according to my sentence.'

Kidd's offer was ignored, and he duly went to his fate. Opinion at the time, shared by some experts now, was that the letter was a bluff. However, several powerful people in 18th-century England stood to benefit if Kidd, guilty or innocent, were silenced forever.

The Kidd legend flourished after his death. Then, more than 200 years later, in 1929, came the first solid piece of evidence that he may not have been bluffing after all. Hubert Palmer, a retired lawyer living in Eastbourne, England, bought a 17th-century oak desk bearing the inscription 'Captain William Kidd – Adventure Galley 1699'. Searching for secret compartments, Palmer accidentally broke one of the runners of the flap; inside he found a narrow brass tube with a parchment map wrapped around it. The map showed an island described as being in the China Sea, initialed 'WK' and dated 1699. Over the next five years, Palmer obsessively hunted down other relics of Kidd, finding three more maps in the process. All seemed to be of the same place, although the details varied. All seemed to be authentic, with handwriting that matched samples of Kidd's script, kept in the Public Records Office in London.

The discoveries sparked off a series of treasure hunts at various locations on America's eastern seaboard, in the Indian Ocean, and in the Sea of Japan, none of which, so far as is known, has yet yielded Kidd's hoard.

The making of a pirate

To anyone who knew Kidd before 1696, he would have seemed an unlikely candidate for infamy. Born in Scotland about 1645, he served in the English navy during the wars against the Dutch. Afterwards, he became a merchant, developing a successful trade with the Indies and eventually moving to New York, where he married a wealthy widow. Captain and Mrs Kidd moved in the upper echelons of New York society, and a record of 1689 describes him as a 'gentleman'.

But Kidd the merchant and society figure was still Kidd the sea captain. Between 1689 and 1695, he several times commanded a privateer, a private armed vessel licensed to harry the King's enemies – in this case, the French. At this time, it seems, Kidd had no thoughts of becoming a pirate. Indeed, his first privateer, the *Blessed William,* was stolen by his mutinous crew while it was undergoing repairs in Antigua. The men sailed off to raid shipping on their own account, but Kidd did not join them.

By 1695, the English government considered that pirates operating in the Atlantic and Indian oceans posed more of a threat to merchant shipping than the French did. But with England still at war with France, the navy could not be spared to rout the pirates out. So the newly appointed Governor of New York, the Earl of Bellomont, and several individual members of the government, including the First Lord of the Admiralty and the Chancellor, agreed on the plan that was eventually to bring Kidd to Execution Dock.

They decided to finance an unofficial expedition against the pirates, in return for secret shares in the booty, and Kidd was appointed to lead it. The veteran captain knew

Articles of Agreement,

Made the 10th Day of *October,* in the Year of our Lord 1695. Between the Right Honourable *RICHARD* Earl of *BELLOMONT* of the one part, and *Robert Levingston* Esq;

AND

Captain William Kid,

Of the other part.

WHEREAS the said Capt. *William Kid* is desirous of obtaining a Commission as Captain of a Private Man of War in order to take Prizes from the King's Enemies, and otherways to annoy them; and whereas certain Persons did some time since depart from *New-England, Rode-Island, New-York,* and other parts in *America* and elsewhere, with an intention to become Pirates, and to commit Spoils and Depredations, against the Laws of Nations, in the *Red-Sea* or elsewhere, and to return with such Goods and Riches as they should get, to certain places by them agreed upon; of which said Persons and Places, the said Capt. *Kid* hath notice, and is desirous to fight with and subdue the said Pirates, as also other Pirates with whom the said Capt. *Kid* shall meet at Sea, in case he be impowered so to do; and whereas it is agreed between the said Parties, That for the purpose aforesaid a good and sufficient Ship, to the liking of the said Capt. *Kid,* shall be forthwith bought, whereof the said Capt. *Kid* is to have the Command. Now these Presents do witness, and it is agreed between the said Parties,

I. That the Earl of *Bellomont* doth covenant and agree, at his proper Charge, to procure from the King's Majesty, or from the Lords Commissioners of the Admiralty (as the Case shall require) one or more Commissions, impowering him the said Capt. *Kid* to act against the King's Enemies, and to take Prizes from them, as a private Man of War in the usual manner; and also to fight with, conquer and subdue Pirates, and to take them and their Goods; with other large and beneficial Powers and Clauses in such Commissions as may be most proper and effectual in such Cases.

II. The said Earl of *Bellomont* doth covenant and agree, That within three Months after the said Capt. *Kid's* departure from *England,* for the purposes in these Presents mentioned, he will procure, at his proper charge, a Grant from the King, to be made to some indifferent and trusty Person, of all such Mechandizes, Goods, Treasure and other things as shall be taken from the said Pirates, or any other Pirate whatsoever, by the said Capt. *Kid,* or by the said Ship, or any other Ship or Ships under his Command.

III. The said Earl doth agree to pay four Fifth parts, the whole in Five parts to be divided, of all Moneys which shall be laid out for the buying such good and sufficient Ship for the purposes aforesaid, together with Rigging and other Apparel and Furniture thereof, and providing the same with competent victualling the said Ship, to be approved of by the said Parties; and the said other one Fifth part of the said Charges of the said Ship to be paid for by the said *Robert Levingston* and *William Kid.*

IV. The said Earl doth agree, That in order to the speedy buying the said Ship, in part of the said four parts of Five of the said Charges, he will pay down the sum of sixteen hundred Pounds, by way of Advance, on or before the sixth day of *November* next ensuing.

V. The said *Robert Levingston* and *William Kid* do jointly and severally covenant and agree, That on and before the sixth day of *November,* when the said Earl of *Bellomont* is to pay the said Sum of sixteen hundred pounds as aforesaid, they will advance and pay down four hundred pounds in part of the Share and Proportion which they are to have in the said Ship.

Far left:
Kidd went to the gallows at London's notorious Execution Dock in May 1701, despite his eve-of-hanging promise to reveal the whereabouts of booty he claimed to have concealed. Kidd's body, like that of many a pirate before him, was afterwards displayed in chains on a gibbet as a visible reminder of the price of crime. This illustration is from *The Pirate's Own Book* (1837), which inspired many a pirate yarn.

Above:
The fateful agreement of 1695 with the Earl of Bellomont eventually brought Kidd to the gallows. In it, Bellomont undertook to obtain for Kidd a commission as a privateer, and to underwrite the captain's expenses in return for a share of the spoils. What Kidd did not know is that Bellomont was acting as front man for a syndicate of highly-placed public figures, including King William III of England.

that Bellomont, who was to get a 60 percent share, was the main promoter. He did not know that his other backers were even more powerful figures, including the king himself, William III, who was to get 10 percent.

For more than a year, Kidd's ship, the *Adventure Galley,* sailed the Atlantic and Indian oceans without taking a significant prize. Wracked by disease and with supplies running low, the crew became mutinous, knowing that their only pay was to be a share of the booty.

Matters came to a head when Kidd declined to attack a Dutch East Indiaman – which he was forbidden to do under his letter of commission, but which the crew by now expected. In the brooding atmosphere, Kidd killed his gunner, whom he suspected of fomenting mutiny, with a blow from an iron-bound bucket.

A fateful decision

The incident seemed to have made up Kidd's mind, and from then on he launched attacks on

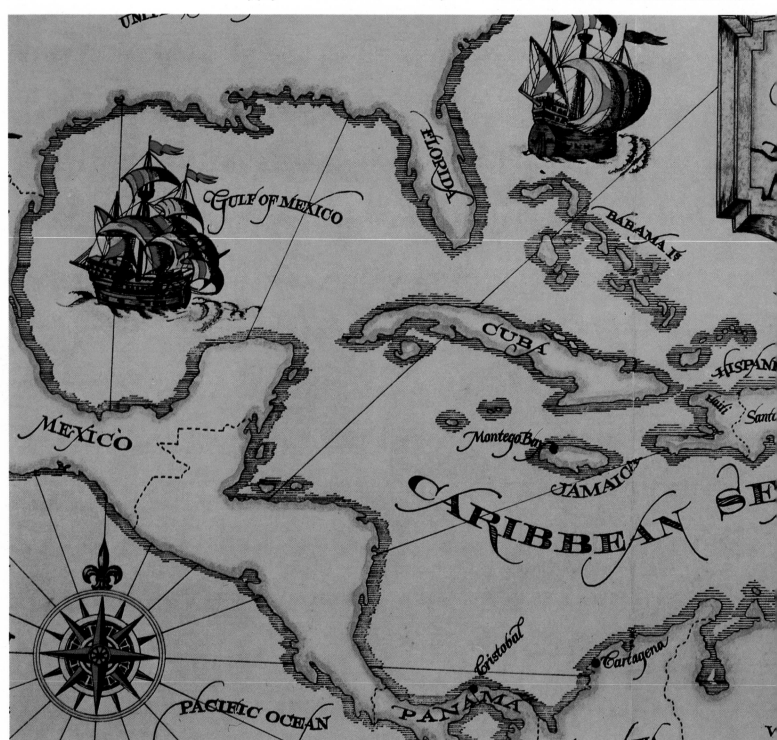

ships and settlements of many nations. His greatest prize was the *Quedah Merchant,* an Armenian vessel commanded by an Englishman and carrying French safe-conduct passes. With the *Quedah Merchant* and another Armenian ship, the *Maiden,* in tow, Kidd sailed to St Mary's Island, near Madagascar, a nest of the very pirates he was supposed to eradicate. There, he was apparently made welcome; the spoils were divided, and Kidd sailed for New York in the *Quedah Merchant,* having

abandoned the *Adventure Galley* as unseaworthy.

Meanwhile, the Admiralty in London had received reports of Kidd's attack on a fellow English captain, albeit of a foreign ship. Kidd was declared a pirate, a fact he learned in the West Indies on the voyage home. He changed vessels again, to the sloop *Antonio,* and made several calls along the American coast before finally putting ashore at Boston. Kidd was apparently expecting protection from Bellomont, but the Governor promptly had him arrested and shipped in irons back to England, where he languished for more than a year in London's Newgate prison before coming to trial.

By that time Bellomont was dead, and both the First Lord of the Admiralty and the Chancellor had been impeached for their part in the expedition. The whole affair had become a scandal threatening the government and even the monarchy. Public opinion had already condemned Kidd, and none of his previous supporters was prepared to risk his position by intervening. His death sentence was almost a foregone conclusion.

Far left:
This pirate-style map of the Caribbean shows the hunting-grounds of the buccaneers of the Spanish Main. By conscious or unconscious irony, the two ships depicted are placed near the sites of famous treasure wrecks.

Below:
Friends in high places did not dare to intervene to save Captain William Kidd when he was arraigned for piracy before the House of Commons in London. He was unable to produce vital evidence on his own behalf and was duly sentenced to death, leaving behind him one of the most enduring stories of hidden pirate gold.

Where is Treasure Island?

Above:
A 19th-century print sold by Pollock's Toy Theatre shop in London purports to show William Kidd in action, but it is a very romanticized portrait. The shop was a favorite browsing spot for Robert Louis Stevenson (1850-94), whose famous novel *Treasure Island* drew on Kidd's real-life career.

Top right:
Two versions of the treasure-map found in the early 20th century and attributed to Kidd. The lower, more detailed version clearly places the island in the China Sea. But letters in the cross-hatching on the left of the island spell out the word 'oak' — perhaps a reference to Oak Island off the coast of Nova Scotia. The writing around the border is assumed to contain instructions on how to locate the treasure, while the cryptic reference to '20 turtles' may be a clue that the map is in fact upside down.

The legend of Captain Kidd's 'treasure island' rapidly gained impetus after his death, and the value of the treasure multiplied into millions, although there is no firm evidence that Kidd acquired much more than the gold, silver, jewelry and silks from the *Quedah Merchant* and the *Maiden* during his brief spell of piracy. Some of that loot was shared out among the crew who remained in Madagascar when Kidd put in there in 1698, and more was given to seamen who left the sloop *Antonio* at Lewes in Delaware Bay before Kidd arrived in Boston in July 1699. We also know that, prior to Kidd's arrival in Boston, he moored at Gardiner's Island, off Long Island, and deposited bales and chests, including at least one containing gold. However, those goods were quickly traced and collected by Lord Bellomont.

Sceptics argue that the original tales of Kidd's treasure grew up around his activities on Gardiner's Island, and were fueled by his eve-of-execution letter. The letter remains the only authenticated primary evidence that the treasure exists at all. The maps found by Palmer all came from genuine sea-chests of Kidd's era, bearing Kidd's name. And the writing on them does appear to match that of Kidd. But, say the sceptics, for one man to discover no fewer than four pirate maps after more than 200 years, stretches coincidence a very long way.

The most explicit of the charts appeared in 1934, inside a chest inscribed 'William and Sarah Kidd, Their Chest'. It gives the latitude and longitude of the island, as well as coded instructions about where the treasure is hidden. But in those days, latitude was not universally calculated from the Greenwich meridian, so the bearings on the chart are of little use. In addition, the code is obscure. Another complicating factor is that the island is clearly stated to be in the China Sea. So far as is known, Kidd did not visit that area during his voyage of 1696-99.

A Japanese discovery

According to one theory, the island may be Yokoate, which is part of a group stretching from southern Japan toward Taiwan. In 1952, some Japanese fishermen took shelter in a bay there. Exploring ashore, they found carvings of a horned animal on a rock face. The discovery eventually came to the attention of the Japanese scholar Nagashima, who remembered that Kidd had sometimes used a stylized drawing of a young goat as his mark – a pun on his surname.

Nagashima investigated the spot, where he is rumored to have found the entrance to a cave almost entirely covered by undergrowth. Inside, it is said, a heap of old iron boxes contained some $50 million in gold and silver coins, which Nagashima had shipped back to Tokyo in conditions of great secrecy. Subsequently, Japanese newspapers reported that Nagashima had vanished, allegedly taking the treasure with him, and was being sought by the police.

Whether or not Nagashima did find Kidd's treasure, there are plenty of people who argue that the China Sea reference on the charts is correct. They contend that the maps, or perhaps a lost original from which they were copied, do not denote a cache actually made by Kidd, but were acquired by him at some stage during his career as a privateer. The theory conveniently explains one mystery – why a prosperous merchant should accept a risky commission to do battle with pirates. Kidd's aim all along, it is said, was to use the opportunity of the *Adventure Galley* voyage to try to find the China Sea island for himself, making and concealing various copies of the chart in case one was lost or stolen.

Those who support this view also say that it explains why Kidd, in his last letter, was not more specific about the location of the treasure – because he did not know it precisely himself. On the other hand, as he was bargaining for his life and by no means a fool, why should he have given full information to his captors until he had secured a promise of mercy?

Other islands

Another school of thought maintains that the China Sea location is merely a blind, intended to put anyone stumbling on the map accidentally off the scent, and that Kidd really buried the treasure much nearer home. The Caribbean is a possible site, as it was there that Kidd abandoned the *Quedah Merchant* in favor

of the *Antonio*. Certainly, in his subsequent dealings with Bellomont, Kidd made much of the treasure that he said he had left on the *Quedah Merchant*. This claim does not ring true because by then the vessel had been reduced to a hulk, and would almost certainly have been looted. If, however, Kidd had concealed the cargo somewhere on the islands, and was using the ship's name as a sort of shorthand for Bellomont, the story would make more sense. But no real evidence has been found to support it.

The most intriguing theory, though, places Kidd's island much farther north, off the coast of Nova Scotia. It is called Oak Island, and it has been under investigation by treasure-seekers since 1804, without yet yielding all its mysteries.

Above:
Another romanticized view of Kidd, this time supervising the burial of treasure on Gardiner's Island, off the coast of New York. Kidd did deposit booty there some time in 1699, but so far as is known all of it was recovered by the authorities soon afterwards.

The puzzle of Panama

Right:
Henry Morgan (?1635-88)
captured the seemingly
impregnable Spanish base of
Panama City in 1670 on behalf of
the British. He stripped it of its
lavish treasures, but when the
spoils came to be shared out there
was little enough for his crew. For
three centuries people have
speculated about what happened
to the rest of Morgan's booty.
Some believe it is buried near
Panama, others that it is hidden on
one of the islands that dot the
Caribbean.

In the 17th century, Panama City was the richest
settlement in the whole of the New World, a
storehouse of gold and silver wrested from the
Incas by their Spanish conquerors. Its vast
wealth had drawn the greedy eyes of privateers
and pirates from Drake's time onwards, but
Panama was heavily defended against seaward
attack from the Pacific, and seemingly protected
by thick jungle against an onslaught by land.
However, the city's defences proved no
match for one of the most notorious raiders
of the Spanish Main, Welsh-born Captain
Henry Morgan.

In 1670, Morgan assembled a fleet of 36 ships
and nearly 2,000 men for the biggest-ever raid
on Spanish territories. Once out from Port
Royal, the force agreed that Panama should be
the target. The fleet anchored off the mouth of
the Chagres River, on the Caribbean side of the
Isthmus of Panama, and Morgan and 1,400
men began the nine-day journey by sea and
land to the Pacific coast.

News of their impending arrival had reached
the Spaniards in Panama, and cavalry and
infantry were mobilized to defend the city.
Unfortunately for Spain, the terrain on which
they chose to fight was unsuitable for cavalry,
and a herd of cattle, which the defenders had
intended to drive into Morgan's battle line,
stampeded and threw the infantry into disarray.
The Spaniards fled, putting Panama itself to
the torch.

Once the flames had died down, Morgan and
his men rampaged through the city in search of
treasure. Eventually the raiders left, taking with
them 175 mules laden with plate, gold and
silver coins, and jewelry, and sowing the seeds
of a mystery that continues to intrigue treasure-
hunters to this day.

The lost fortune

The mule-train, although carrying a fortune, did
not represent anything like the spoils that might
have been expected from Panama. Morgan's
raid had been by land, so Panama's harbor had
not been blockaded, and at least one Spanish
treasure-ship, and possibly others, had escaped.

A large portion of the valuable loot which had
been brought out by mules appeared to have
vanished when the survivors came to share it
out back at their ships. They received just £10 a
head which, even when multiplied a
hundredfold to equal modern values, was a
paltry sum after all their privations. Morgan
himself slipped away on his ship, having

ordered cannon from the captured fort of San Lorenzo to be installed on board. The clear implication was that he had seized the best part of the booty for his own ends.

The English government, which stood to gain a share of the treasure as Morgan was operating as a privateer, clearly believed it had been swindled. On his return to Jamaica, Morgan was arrested and shipped back to England to face charges of piracy. Unlike the luckless William Kidd, however, Morgan was a popular hero. His trial never took place, and he eventually returned to the Caribbean as Lieutenant-Governor of Jamaica, where he became the scourge of English and Spanish pirates alike before dying of drink at the age of 53.

During his lifetime, Morgan made no reference to treasure he had hidden, although his former shipmates did. There are many who believe that the hoard remains to be found somewhere in the Caribbean between Panama and Jamaica.

Far left:
The name of Morgan cast as much fear into the Spanish as that of Drake had done a century earlier. In this 18th-century engraving, Morgan (left foreground) is depicted leading the sack of Port-au-Prince (Puerto del Principe), a Spanish settlement in Cuba.

Above:
In this 17th-century map of the Isthmus of Panama, north is at the bottom, and the Pacific Ocean appears at the top. Morgan's raiders landed on the Caribbean coast, and made their way south towards Panama City (top left) along the Chagre, the river that meanders across the center of the map. Their perilous journey took them nine days. Their aim was to surprise Spanish defenders of Panama City, who were not accustomed to attacks from land. But the Spanish learned in advance they were coming, and incompetence, rather than surprise, caused Panama to fall.

The Coco Island hoards

As early as 1683 one area of what is now Costa Rican territory began to earn a reputation as a potential source of incalculable wealth, a reputation it still possesses today. The area is the Ile del Coco, an island 300 miles southwest of the Costa Rican mainland, in the Pacific. There, at least three, and possibly several more, pirate hoards are known to have been concealed.

Among the first of the pirates to take advantage of it was the Englishman Captain Edward Davis, one of a group of notorious buccaneers whose other members included John Coxon, Bartholomew Sharp, and William Dampier. The last-named later gained respectability as a navigator and writer, who sailed round the world three times. Some of these high-spirited adventurers were as ignorant and careless as they were brave.

Davis was shrewder than most of his colleagues. In his ship, *Bachelor's Delight,* he emerged periodically from Coco to prey on Spanish vessels and coastal towns such as Guayaquil in Ecuador. The biggest prize of all, the Lima treasure-fleet, eluded him, because a French force with which he allied himself stood off while Davis unsuccessfully took on the Spaniards. However, he amassed enough booty to retire temporarily to Florida during King James II's amnesty for pirates, before taking up piracy again and disappearing mysteriously about 1702.

Bonito's bonanza

The remote island also provided a suitable hideaway for another pirate, more than 100 years after Davis' presumed death, the Portuguese Benito Bonito. In 1819, Bonito plundered a cargo of gold from the Mexican port of Acapulco and, returning to Coco, hid it in Wafer Bay. Two years later, the pirate was killed in an engagement with a British man-o'-war in the West Indies, so he could not reclaim his treasure.

Unlike Davis, however, Bonito left clues to the whereabouts of the cache. In 1880, the grandson of one of the men who had sailed with Bonito revealed a treasure-map to a German sailor called Gissler. It showed an island which the old pirate had called 'Las Palmas'. Gissler copied the map and, eight years later in Hawaii, came across another map. By comparison, he concluded that the island in question was Coco. He eventually settled on Coco and spent 20 years there searching for the treasure. During that time he went through considerable hardship, including a raid by two English cruisers bent on seizing any booty for themselves. The English found nothing, and Gissler was not much luckier. All he had to show for two decades of effort was one Spanish doubloon dated 1788, and he died penniless in New York in 1930.

By a supreme irony, Bonito's hoard was located just two years after Gissler's death, by treasure-seekers using the newly invented metal detector. The gold was found more or less where the maps showed it would be – proof that at least some reputed pirate charts are accurate.

Looking for Thompson's haul

The location of the third, and potentially most valuable, of the Coco treasures was also plotted on a map, drawn on his deathbed by the Scotsman William Thompson, the man who originally hid it. This cache – part of the vast wealth amassed by the Spanish civil and religious authorities during nearly three centuries' occupation of Peru – is the biggest attraction on Coco for treasure-seekers.

Left:
At least two hoards are thought to be buried on Ile del Coco (Cocos Island), probably somewhere at the northern tip in the area around Wafer Bay and Chatham Bay. It was there that, in 1932, treasure-seekers using a metal detector found gold concealed in the 19th century by the buccaneer Benito Bonito. The island's biggest prize, priceless treasure removed from Lima in Peru in 1823, has yet to yield itself up.

Far left:
Dense shrubs cover most of the Ile del Coco in the Pacific, a pirates' hideaway from the 17th to the 19th century.

COCOS ISLAND
(densely covered with trees and bushes)

NORTH PACIFIC OCEAN
COCOS ISLAND

Left:
A fanfare of publicity accompanied the British expedition to the Ile del Coco in 1932. This map is extracted from a feature in the *Illustrated London News* of the time. Other forays to the island have been conducted in far greater secrecy.

Our Lady of Lima

In 1823, the revolutionary armies of Simón Bolívar were driving the Spaniards from the South American empire they had built up over the previous three centuries. The liberator's forces were drawing near to Lima, capital of the viceroyalty of Peru and one of the wealthiest cities on the continent, throwing civil and church authorities into panic.

William Thompson's brig, the *Mary Dear,* lay at anchor in the port of Lima after a trade voyage, and the Spaniards, desperate to save their fortunes, quickly struck a deal with the captain. The *Mary Dear* was to take aboard a quantity of treasure, under Spanish guard, to prevent its falling into Bolívar's hands. If the city held out successfully against the revolutionaries, Thompson was to return with his cargo in a few weeks. If Lima capitulated, Thompson was to set a course for Panama City, then still a Spanish bastion, and offload the treasure there.

The precious items were transferred to the brig, and they represented a fortune, including a lifesize statue of the Madonna, crafted in solid gold. The *Mary Dear* swiftly slipped anchor... But from the start, Thompson appears to have had no intention of observing his side of the bargain. Once at sea, he quickly disposed of the Spanish guards and headed for the Ile del Coco. Ashore, the bulk of the treasure was concealed in a cave, and the rest shared out among Thompson's crew. But they were not to enjoy their new found prosperity for long.

The Spaniards were not as trusting as they seemed, and Thompson was already under suspicion. The *Mary Dear* was captured by the frigate *Espiègle* and all hands, except for Thompson and the first mate, were put to death for theft and piracy. Those two were spared to guide the Spaniards to the main cache.

Back on Coco, the two men managed to elude their captors and hide while a fruitless search for the treasure was carried out. After a week, the Spaniards gave up and set sail, leaving Thompson and the mate marooned with their spoils. Another week went by before a whaler put into the island. The two buccaneers revealed themselves, though not the existence of the treasure, and were carried to safety.

The tell-tale map

The mate died, perhaps as the result of his ordeal, leaving Thompson the only man alive who knew the precise whereabouts of the Lima treasure. But try as he would, the Scotsman could not raise the money to return and claim it. In his later years, Thompson befriended a wandering seaman called John Keating, and it was to Keating that Thompson, on his deathbed, gave the treasure-map.

Keating was luckier than Thompson had been. He soon found a financial backer to accompany him to Coco, and between them

Far right:
Since the 1870s, the Ile del Coco has been the destination of dozens of treasure-hunting expeditions. This British team visited the island aboard SS *Vigilant* in 1932.

they located the cave, removing what they could carry in their pockets. Unfortunately, Keating's crew realized what was afoot and threatened to kill him unless he revealed the site of the cave. But Keating, like Thompson before him, escaped and hid. The crew searched for the treasure in vain, then left. Keating was picked up by a passing ship months later.

In 1875, a seaman called Bob Flower slipped through the undergrowth into a pit while exploring the island. Fearing for his life, he managed to scramble out quickly, but not before noticing some gold coins. When Flower came to retrace the spot, he could not find it. Subsequent expeditions retrieved some items – a gold Madonna, 2 feet high, from the Bay of Hope, and 133 gold and silver coins from the same area. All the evidence, however, suggests there is plenty more treasure to come to light.

Clues to the cache

One of the problems facing prospectors is knowing exactly what kind of site they are looking for. The cave features in the earliest records, but Keating also mentioned a stone with a letter K carved on it, and an arrow pointing to a hollow tree. The stone and tree – with a cable and hook attached to it – were traced around the turn of the century, but no sign of the treasure was found.

The mysterious money pit

Right:
In 1970, the Triton salvage company launched the biggest onslaught yet on the money pit, using modern mining techniques. Three old chests were apparently located, but further information about the excavation was withheld.

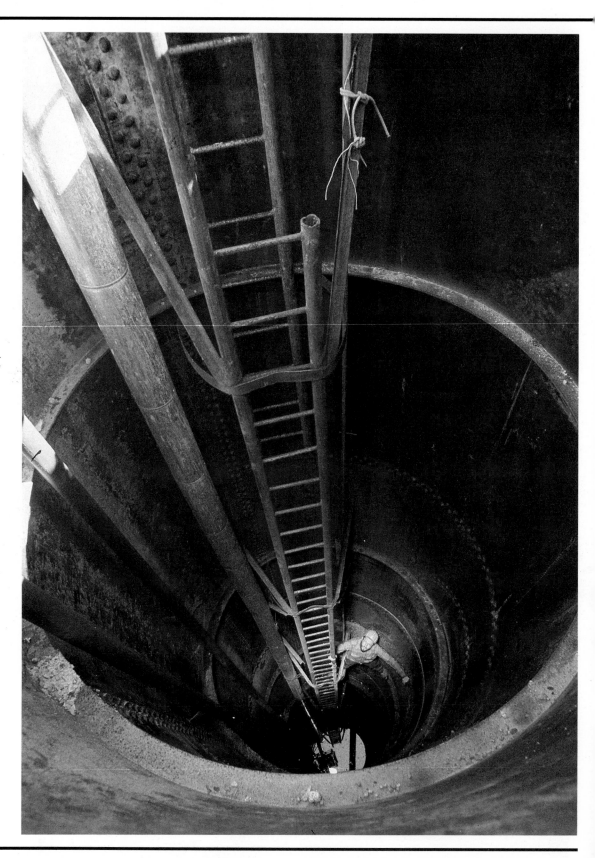

Little Oak Island lies four miles off the coast of Nova Scotia, sheltered from the open ocean by other islands to seaward. At its eastern end, a natural shaft or blowhole apparently once led downward to a large cavern some 200 feet below the surface. The shaft has been blocked by a series of platforms and partially flooded through side tunnels to create a virtually inaccessible 'money pit' that, according to local legend, contains a massive store of treasure.

Almost certainly, the island was used as a haven by pirates in the 17th and 18th centuries, and inevitably it has become linked with the name of Captain Kidd. But there are flaws in the tales linking Kidd to Oak. It is just possible that the *Antonio* could have reached the island in its wanderings along the Atlantic coast before Kidd came ashore at Boston, but it is certain that he would not have had time then to prepare the complex money pit. Other possibilities remain. The pit may have already been in existence, simply waiting for Kidd to install his treasure and seal it; but that is unlikely, again because of time. The pit may have been prepared on some other occasion, by Kidd or someone else. Or Kidd may indeed have visited Oak in 1699, but hidden his treasure on an entirely different site.

The making of the pit

Whoever constructed the money pit was an engineer of great ability. The system of tunnels and platforms is arranged in such a way that anyone trying to reach the lowest platform, on which the treasure is presumed to rest, cannot do so without flooding the shaft entirely with seawater unless the tunnels, deep in the ground, can be dammed first.

The earliest records of possible pirate activity on Oak Island date from 1763, when residents in the settlement of Chester, across the bay, noticed 'strange lights and fires'. However, no one investigated, and it was not until 1795 that the money pit was discovered. A 16-year-old boy exploring the island noticed a circular depression in the ground and, with two friends, began to dig. The boys uncovered one platform of stone and two of logs before giving up. Nine years later, having found financial backers, the three returned and dug down to a depth of 98 feet before seawater flooded in.

Digging continues

In the 1840s, a syndicate was formed to excavate the pit by digging a new shaft parallel to the original. These efforts were equally

unsuccessful, and the second shaft also flooded. For two years from 1909, Captain Harry L Boudouin of New York tried his hand at excavation. His team was eventually forced to give up, and he declared in disgust, 'There was never a pirate or any other treasure in the money pit on Oak Island.' But his disappointment did not deter others, and a series of further expeditions visited the site.

By 1967, the depredations of the treasure-hunters had so churned up the eastern end of the island that all surface clues had disappeared in a sea of mud. However, one possibly significant piece of evidence was discovered – a stone dated 1704.

In 1970, a salvage company, Triton, launched the biggest onslaught on the money pit to date. Using modern equipment, the excavators plumbed the pit to a depth of 212 feet, some 40 feet lower than anyone had previously reached, and revealed the existence of the cave at the base of the shaft. Underwater cameras showed old logs piled on the cave floor and, it was said, three chests and a human hand apparently chopped off at the wrist.

First among the unanswered questions is who built the pit, and when? The earliest evidence of activity is the dated stone, which seems to rule out a link with Kidd, because he had been dead for three years by 1704. But the pit may have been dug much later, in 1763, when the citizens of Chester noticed the strange lights. Yet the intriguing possibility that Kidd visited the island and hid treasure there, either before or after his last disastrous voyage, still exists.

Left:
A sign at Smith's Cove tells the sad story of a failed attempt on the money pit in 1965. Four men died in the attempt to pump it dry.

Overleaf:
In this view of Little Oak Island, Nova Scotia, from the south, its shape can clearly be seen to resemble that on the treasure-maps attributed to William Kidd. The existence of the money pit on Oak Island was already known when the maps began to appear earlier this century.

Chapter 2

Abandon Ship

The quest for pirate gold is one of the most romantic aspects of treasure-hunting, but such gold is an elusive commodity. Almost as romantic, and far less elusive, are the wrecks littering the world's shipping lanes and coastal waters. For centuries, the approximate locations of major shipwrecks have been recorded – in particular if the vessels involved were carrying precious cargoes, or were symbols of national pride such as great warships or ocean liners.

The Nanking Cargo

In April 1986, Amsterdam was the venue for one of the biggest auctions of rediscovered treasure in history. It was not, however, a hoard of precious metals or cache of stolen jewels that brought collectors from all over the world to Holland, but 100,000 pieces of antique Chinese porcelain. After over 200 years at the bottom of the China Sea, the Nanking Cargo, as it had become known, had finally reached its destination.

Carefully packed into crates of tea, the porcelain had been the main cargo of a Dutch East Indiaman. The merchant ship, which remains unidentified, was on its homeward voyage from Canton to Europe sometime in the 1750s. Unfortunately disaster struck and the ship went to the bottom, though by some miracle not violently enough to disturb its fragile cargo. Sealed like a time-capsule beneath the waters for 200 years, the contents of the ship's hold remained intact and in mint condition, transforming the porcelain from simple

commodities of 18th-century commerce to treasure worth discovering.

It was rediscovered in the 1980s by British salvage expert Captain Michael Hatcher, a specialist on wrecks in the waters of the Far East. Hatcher was no stranger to delicate salvage operations, having discovered by accident in 1983 the wreck of a 17th-century Asian trading junk. The recovery of the cargo of this vessel revealed an astonishing 23,000 pieces of antique Chinese porcelain from the Ming period, in perfect condition.

The financial rewards for the salvage of such a treasure were brought home to Hatcher when the cargo (which has since become known as the Hatcher collection) was sold at auction for over $2 million!

Inspired by this success, and aided by Swiss-born surveyor Max de Rham, Hatcher began the search for other wrecks which culminated in the successful location and recovery of the Nanking Cargo in 1985.

The treasure itself is remarkable not only for the fact that it has been recovered in such pristine condition, but that so much of it has survived. The quantities are huge and display a dazzling variety. There are, for example, more than 40,000 tea bowls and saucers and enough tableware to assemble complete dinner services of more than 370 pieces with settings for 140 guests.

Attractive porcelain is all very well, of course, but included in the finds is a group of objects to whet the appetites of those who like their sunken treasure of a little more traditional

Left:
Attempts at salvage are nothing new, as this 18th-century picture shows. William Tracy of Portsea tried in 1783 to raise the warship *Royal George* from the waters of Spithead, the naval anchorage in the Solent off Portsmouth in southern England.

Chinese porcelain of the 18th century and gold bars formed part of the cargo of a Dutch East Indiaman, recovered off the China coast by Captain Hatcher in 1985, and commanded sky-high prices at auction in early 1986. Porcelain was often packed in with tea in ships returning from the East, an efficient way to protect it against breakage.

kind; because Hatcher and his team also discovered gold.

In a small area just outside the hull of the wreck, divers discovered 125 gold ingots of two extremely rare Chinese types: the first, a series of cup-shaped ingots known as 'Nanking Shoes'; the second, a group of small rectangular ingots, about four inches long. Since no 18th-century Chinese gold of these types is known in the West, this particular find is worth as much perhaps for its historical value as for its value as bullion.

The earliest wrecks

In 1984, underwater archaeologists working off the Mediterranean coast of Turkey released details of an amazing find – the well-preserved wreck of a merchant ship that had plied the seas some 3,400 years ago, while Tutankhamun ruled Egypt and before the ancient Greeks had fought the Trojan War. The nationality of the vessel is not known, but its cargo of Bronze Age goods showed that it had voyaged between Greece, Cyprus, and the lands of the early Phoenicians. To date, it is the earliest shipwreck found.

The meticulously excavated ship stirred the imagination of archaeologists, if not that of the general public. Its load of pottery and wine jars, although of considerable archaeological importance, could not match the more glamorous treasures dredged up from later wrecks such as those of Spanish plate-galleons or England's *Mary Rose.* Even so, it demonstrated two highly significant things: seawater, seabed silt, and marine accretions such as barnacles and weeds are remarkable preservatives of many ancient materials and artifacts; and underwater currents do not move items on the seabed nearly as much as had once been believed.

Those early wrecks that have been thoroughly excavated, such as the one off Turkey, have not been found to contain treasure in the conventional sense of the word. In most cases, their contents consisted of pottery, wine-jars, bronze goods, and marble in various stages of working – all of great interest to historians and archaeologists, but of little intrinsic value.

Precious items are generally lacking, too, in wrecks dating from the fall of Rome to the 15th century – for example, the five 11th-century ships raised at Roskilde in Denmark, the Venetian galley of about 1439 discovered in Italy's Lake Garda, and the 12th-century boat which was one of an incredible 156 vessels found when part of the Zuider Zee in Holland was drained in the 1950s. Possible exceptions are two Viking longships that went down somewhere off the Shetland Islands while returning to Norway after a series of raids in

1151. They are said to be laden with gold and silver, but have never been found. However, it is only when we reach the 16th century, the beginnings of the great age of European exploration and conquest, that the true quest for treasure lost under water gets under way.

Wrecks of the Spanish Main

The golden era of piracy was born with Columbus's voyages to the New World, and the same might also be said of shipwrecks. For the richly-laden vessels that drew the attention of the sea-raiders were susceptible to other perils of the deep – currents, storms, rocks, reefs, and shallows. Nowhere was this more true than in the Caribbean and adjoining waters of the

Above:
Amphorae (wine jars) are among the artifacts most frequently retrieved from ancient Greek and Roman wrecks in the Mediterranean. The area, like the Caribbean, is a favorite hunting-ground for underwater explorers because of relatively high temperatures and good visibility, at least close to the coast.

Above:
The wreckage of the Swedish flagship *Kronan*, 28 meters below the surface of the Baltic, where she was sunk in 1676 by the combined action of the Dutch and Danish navies. Work on excavating the 2,140-ton vessel began in 1981 in considerable secrecy, for fear that undersea looters might locate the precise site of the wreck and strip it of historically valuable artifacts. Because of low oxygen in the water, the *Kronan's* huge bronze cannons – 128 in all – were remarkably well preserved. Other finds include the anchor, a ship's bell and the compass.

Atlantic, the region loosely known as the Spanish Main.

The first great wreck of a Spanish treasure-fleet in the Caribbean consisted of 32 caravels, including the flagship *El Dorado,* that set sail from Hispaniola in July 1502 despite warnings from Christopher Columbus himself of an impending hurricane. Aboard the *El Dorado* were Admiral Antonio de Torres, Governor Bobadilla of Hispaniola, an estimated $2 million in gold and silver, and a solid gold table said to weigh 3,000 lb – Bobadilla's gift to the King and Queen of Spain. Columbus, who had just returned from Spain, watched helplessly as the vessels put to sea. Three days out, in the Mona Passage between the Dominican Republic and Puerto Rico, the hurricane struck, destroying the *El Dorado* and 25 other ships. The wrecks

of some were later found on the reefs and beaches of the passage, but 17 have never been traced, among them the *El Dorado* with its precious table.

Bad weather struck a Spanish plate fleet in 1553 off Padre Island in what is now Texas. Out of 20 vessels, only three survived, and those shipwrecked sailors not drowned were slaughtered by hostile Indians ashore, whose presence is thought to have deterred contemporary efforts at salvage.

The Padre Island disaster was, in terms of ships and cargoes lost, one of the three biggest to hit a Spanish plate fleet. The other two occurred in 1715 and 1733, both off the Florida Keys. The tracing and salvage of vessels from the 1715 fleet is one of the most inspiring examples of amateur but responsible treasure-

Silt accumulated over wrecks is a perennial problem for salvagers, although it also helps to preserve material. This so-called 'clam dredger' was developed before World War I to help in the clearance of underwater sites.

SUBMARINE TUBE BUILT OF STEEL PLATING AND HINGED WITHIN HULL OF SURFACE-VESSEL

LENGTH 86 FEET DIAMETER 5 FT

A - WORKING COMPARTMENT FOR WHEELING IN PARALLEL LINES.

B & C - RAKES ROTATED AND ELEVATED BY MACHINERY WITHIN THE CHAMBER MARKED A.

D. CAR RUNNING ON RAILS ON OUTER SURFACE OF TUBE. INTO THIS CAR THE OYSTERS AND OTHER CONTENTS OF THE RAKES ARE DUMPED. IT IS THEN HAULED TO THE SURFACE

TUBE

THE CLAM DREDGER.

SAND PUMP

WORKING CHAMBER FITTED WITH OBSERVATION PORTS AND SEARCH LIGHTS

Below:
Divers working on the wreck of an ancient merchant ship off Bodrum, on the coast of Turkey, carry baskets of recovered artifacts to a submerged decompression chamber in preparation for returning to the surface.

Far right:
This gold dish, now on display in Key West, Florida, is part of the fabulous treasure recovered in the 1980s from the Spanish plate-vessel *Nuestra Señora de Atocha,* which foundered in a hurricane in 1622. The galleon was en route from Havana to Spain when she was wrecked off the Florida Keys.

hunting, yielding large quantities of valuable artifacts. To date, finds from the 1733 fleet have been relatively disappointing, probably because it was wrecked in very shallow water. The presumed remains of the flagship, the *Rui,* were located in 1949, but earlier divers had not left much – some gold and silver coins, weapons, jewelry, and a silver statue of a dancer.

Losses increase
By the early part of the 17th century, sea traffic between the New World and Spain and, to a much lesser extent, Portugal, was at its height and so were the numerical losses of ships. In 1605, four galleons went down on the Serranilla Bank, midway between Central America and Jamaica. The Spaniards spent 60 years trying to find them and raise their cargoes, without success. In 1622, at least 15 vessels foundered along the Florida Keys from the Dry Tortugas. Among them were the *Nuestra Señora de Atocha* and the *La Margarita,* near the Marquesa islets off Key West.

Both these vessels were the objects of a 16-year, almost obsessive quest by the American treasure-hunter Mel Fisher. His tenacity was rewarded in 1985, when divers located the *Atocha* and reported that she contained precious artifacts, coins, and bullion worth an estimated $450 million, the most valuable haul ever retrieved from a ship of the period. Using side-scanning sonar and suction-pipes to clear sand and silt, Fisher's team uncovered a massive pile of silver bars, treasure-chests of gold doubloons and silver pieces-of-eight, and exquisite jewelry. Some will be sold to collectors, and the rest displayed in a museum at Key West.

A year after the *Atocha* was lost, two other Spanish galleons also foundered off Florida, near Ais. The *Santissima Trinidad* went down slowly enough for passengers, crew, and cargo to be taken off, but the *Espiritu Santo el Mayor* sank with the loss of all her treasure and 250 lives.

In 1628, the treasure-fleets suffered their most humiliating blow, when Dutch warships drove 24 of the vessels ashore at Matanzas Bay and ransacked most of what they were carrying. And in 1632, a hurricane caused almost equal losses, wrecking 19 galleons along the Mexican coast from the Bajo de las Arcas to Tabasco. In addition to gold and silver, they were carrying cochineal, silk, brazilwood, and indigo.

Two Caribbean wrecks from later in the 17th century show the widely varying successes of salvage divers of the era. The *Nuestra Señora de la Concepción,* another hurricane victim, came to grief on the Silver Bank north of Hispaniola in 1641. About 40 years later, an English expedition financed by King Charles II

Above:
A platinum ingot, worth around $200,000, salvaged by Japanese divers is displayed to the world's press in 1980. It came from a wreck found off the Japanese island of Tsushima, believed to be that of the Tsarist cruiser *Admiral Nakhimov.* The *Nakhimov* went down in 1905 in a sea battle during the Russo-Japanese war. She was used by Tsar Nicholas II as a 'floating bank', and was reputedly carrying gold and platinum worth $3,000 million at present values when she sank.

and led by one William Phips, set about raising her cargo of silver, using a diving-bell to create an air pocket from which the divers could breathe. Some 34 tons of treasure were recovered, earning Phips a knighthood and the governership of Massachusetts. By contrast, when the *Nuestra Señora de las Maravillas* collided with another galleon on the Little Bahama Bank, local divers could recover only 1.5 million pesos' worth of the 5 million pesos of treasure. The rest, so far as is known, is still there, covered by the shifting sands.

By the middle of the 18th century, the great days of the Spanish plate fleets were over, and the reports of lost treasure tend to involve single ships such as the *Invencible,* struck by lightning in Havana harbor while carrying a cargo valued at 4 million pesos, and the British warship *Tay,* with treasure to the value of 2 million pesos, which was wrecked on the Alacran Reef off Mexico in 1816. So far as is known, neither has been salvaged.

Treacherous fringes of the Atlantic
The waters of the Caribbean may be a veritable paradise for undersea treasure-seekers, but other areas of the Atlantic north of the Equator offer almost as much in lost riches. Its fringes, including the English Channel and the North Sea, are a graveyard of shipping – in particular, the eastern seaboard of North America, Ireland, the Orkneys and Shetlands, the Isles of Scilly, and the stretch of ocean bounded to the west by the Azores, Madeira, and the Canaries, and to the east by Portugal and Spain.

The last of these is particularly enticing, for it represents the final stage of the voyage for Portuguese vessels returning laden from Brazil and the East Indies, for the survivors of Spanish plate fleets bound from the New World and, later, for British, French, and Dutch merchantmen heading for English Channel and North Sea ports. According to one informed estimate, a small portion of this area – around the mouth of the Guadalquivir River in Spain –

Queenstown, 7. Mai 1915.
Der Cunardampfer „Lusitania" ist torpediert worden und gesunken.

contains between 500 and 600 wrecks, few of which have yet been pinpointed, let alone salvaged. Treasures outshining even those of the *Atocha* may be there for the finding.

Between the Iberian peninsula and the Azores, the waters enjoy an eerie reputation almost equal to that of the Bermuda Triangle. There, the first man to sail around the world single-handed, Joshua Slocum, reported that in 1895 his boat had been guided by the ghost of one of Columbus's pilots. There, too, the deserted *Mary Celeste* was discovered in 1872. Although the *Mary Celeste* was not carrying treasure in the normal sense, and indeed her cargo was virtually intact, her lifeboats, navigation books and equipment, and ship's papers were missing, and would be worth a fortune if ever found.

The Azores and Madeira were welcome sights to seamen nearing the end of a long Atlantic voyage, but another group of islands, far to the north, presented a hazard that most ships'

captains would prefer not to have to face, even today. They are the Scillies, off the southwest tip of England. With the coasts of Devon and Cornwall nearby, they have probably claimed more vessels than any other region of the eastern Atlantic – most dramatically in recent years the oil-tanker *Torrey Canyon,* which came to grief on the Seven Stones Reef in 1967. Nowadays, this region is one of the favorite European hunting-grounds for both professional and amateur treasure-seekers.

In the period from 1641 to 1743, no fewer than seven treasure-ships sank off the Scillies, of which the best known is the *Association,* rediscovered in1967. Four others have also been traced since then. The *Princesse Maria,* a Dutch East Indiaman carrying pieces-of-eight and mercury, went down near Silver Carn in 1686; she was extensively plundered at the time, with King James II taking a share of the spoils, but some valuable artifacts remained when she was relocated in 1973.

Above:
The British liner *Lusitania* was sunk without warning off the south coast of Ireland by a German torpedo on May 7, 1915 – an event commemorated in this contemporary German postcard. Out of nearly 1200 people who died in the wreck, more than 100 were Americans, and the sinking helped to bring the USA into World War I. Salvagers have been working on the site since the 1960s without finding either the gold the ship was reputedly carrying or the priceless art collection that was known to be aboard.

Right:
The sinking of the unarmed *Lusitania* unleashed waves of emotion and hostility on both sides of the Atlantic. The authorities were not above capitalizing on popular feeling to boost enlistment, as this recruiting poster shows.

At the northern end of the British Isles, the Shetlands, with their treacherous reefs called *skerries,* pose as great a threat to shipping as the Scillies do in the south. Until the 19th century, ships other than those plying locally tended to avoid them. However, in some circumstances vessels chose to round Britain by the northerly route rather than risk the English Channel and the Straits of Dover, particularly if they belonged to a nation at war with England or France. That was the course picked by the survivors of the defeated Spanish Armada in 1588.

The rugged coasts of Ireland and Wales are fruitful grounds for treasure-hunters. At least six ships from the Armada have been traced off Ireland, leaving perhaps 10 more still to be located. There are also many wrecks along the Irish coast dating from the 19th century, when transatlantic traffic was reaching its peak and many emigrants were seeking a new life in North America.

However, three ships in particular have attracted enormous attention from salvagers in this area. The earliest, in date order, was the steamship *Royal Charter,* which foundered off Moelfre on the Isle of Anglesey in 1859 while returning from Australia with miners who had made their fortunes in the goldfields there. About 400 people died, many of them trying to swim ashore with their valuables. Coins and jewelry are still being washed up on local beaches. It is generally believed that a substantial amount of bullion is still aboard.

The second is the Cunard liner *Lusitania,* torpedoed in St George's Channel in 1915 in a disaster surpassed in 20th-century maritime lore only by the sinking of the *Titanic.* Out of nearly 2,000 people aboard, 1,198 perished. According to rumor, the *Lusitania* was carrying gold worth $6 million, but there is no firm evidence of that. Since the late 1960s, salvagers have been working on the wreck, and have raised items valued at $4 million, including some of the propellers and the ship's bell, though without finding the gold.

The third is the *Laurentic,* a liner converted into an armed cruiser, sunk by a mine off Lough

Above:
The development of the aqualung has revolutionized underwater excavation since the 1940s. These divers are working on the wreck of a Spanish vessel off the coast of Cuba.

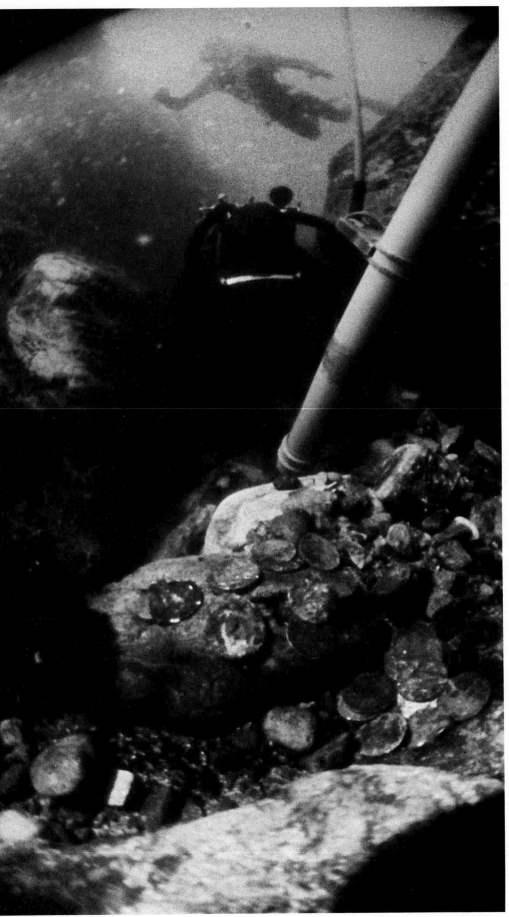

Swilly in Ireland in 1917. She was carrying gold ingots to Canada to pay for war supplies for Britain. Again officially, virtually all of the gold was recovered in the years immediately after the wreck.

Coasts of the Americas

The waters from Florida to the mouth of the Orinoco River undoubtedly conceal the biggest concentration of unrecovered undersea treasure in the Americas, and probably the world. However, there are some magnificent prizes still awaiting finders elsewhere on both Atlantic and Pacific coasts. Among them are nine ships from the Spanish plate fleet of 1750 which strayed much farther north than was customary. Four went down off Cape Hatteras in North Carolina, and three more off Cape Charles in Virginia, in a hurricane.

North of Cape Hatteras, the Atlantic becomes even more perilous, with icebergs and fog adding to the hazards in winter. Fog played a part in the sinking of the liner *Anglo Saxon* off Cape Race, Newfoundland – a notorious ships' graveyard – in 1863, and may have contributed to the collision that sank the *American Republic* some 60 miles off Nantucket in 1909. The *American Republic* was reputedly carrying gold coins with a face value of $3 million and worth about $500 million today. In 1985, salvagers announced plans to retrieve them.

On the Pacific coast of the Americas, two wrecks in particular are intriguing to treasure-hunters. The Spanish warship *Leocadia* foundered off Punta Santa Elena in Ecuador in 1800 with a large quantity of treasure on board. Much of it was reportedly salvaged at the time, but more is said to await a finder. So far as is known, salvage efforts have been less successful on the paddle-steamer *Golden Gate,* which caught fire and sank near Manzanillo in Mexico in 1862. She was carrying $1.6 million in gold coin, of which little was retrieved.

Waters of the South

In the 17th and 18th centuries, England, France, Holland, and Denmark set up companies to trade with the East Indies, previously the virtual domain of the Portuguese among European powers. Their ships plied routes around the Cape of Good Hope and across the Indian Ocean to India itself, the Chinese Empire, the Indonesian islands of Java and Sumatra, Japan, and Australia. As an offshoot of this, a flourishing trade also developed in shipping slaves from Africa to the Americas, in exchange for gold, silver, spices, sugar, and coffee, which were brought back to Europe.

Between 1650 and about 1800, the ships used on the East Indies routes grew dramatically in size, from about 500 tons to 1,000 tons or more. At their peak, these East Indiamen could

Far left:
Divers at work on the Dutch East Indiaman *De Liefde,* wrecked off the Shetland Islands in 1711, reveal a cache of coins amid the wreckage. Efforts were first made to salvage the vessel as long ago as 1712 and are still continuing.

Left:
Some of the coins recovered from the *De Liefde.* She was known to have been carrying a fortune in coin and bullion, but little of it has yet been found.

Above:
The Alvin two-man deep-water search and recovery submarine is an example of the advanced technology that is helping salvagers to locate and recover material from open-ocean sites that could not be reached even a few years ago.

Right:
This amphora (wine jar) on the sea bed is encrusted with corals and is the haunt of tropical fish.

complete the journey from China to northern Europe in about 20 months. Unlike their counterparts trading with the Americas, they were more likely to be carrying treasure in the form of gold, silver, and jewels on the outward trip, to purchase the spices, porcelain, and tea that they brought home, or to pay those who manned their outposts. To some extent, that changed with the discovery of the Australian goldfields in the mid-19th century.

Australian wrecks
In 1629, several ships belonging to the Dutch East India Company were wrecked on a reef in the Wallabi group of islands, off Western Australia. Among them was the *Batavia*, with a cargo that included jewels and silver coin. Some of the men from the ship took a boat and what treasure they could salvage, and made for Java, leaving about 250 passengers and crew behind to await their return with a rescue ship. When they eventually got back to the Wallabis, it was to find that a small group had massacred the rest

of the party, in the hope of carrying off the remaining valuables. The ringleaders were eventually hanged. In 1972, excavation of the *Batavia* began, and items recovered included a large selection of silverware, as well as more than a dozen cannon. It seems likely that other valuable material, from the *Batavia* and from her accompanying ships, is still on the reef.

The discovery of the Australian goldfields gave rise to one of the most bizarre stories of treasure lost at sea in the southern hemisphere, or anywhere else for that matter – the disappearance of the *Starry Crown*. She set sail from Melbourne for London about 1850, carrying passengers and a ton of Australian gold, only to vanish, presumed lost. Some 20 years later, the whaler *Swordfish* was blown off course and became trapped in Antarctic pack ice. Most of the crew died as their provisions dwindled. Soon, only five were left alive.

As *Swordfish* shifted in the ice, another trapped ship came into view. Two of the *Swordfish* crew, one of them the second mate, Last, went on board and found the mystery ship was the *Starry Crown,* deserted, with most of its boats gone, but with plenty of provisions – and the gold intact. Having no means of moving the gold, Last left it where it was. Eventually, he was rescued with the other members of the crew, all of whom died on the voyage back to Melbourne, leaving Last the sole possessor of the secret. He eventually shared it with a man called Manton, and together they plotted a return to Antarctica aboard Manton's ship, the *Black Dog.* She, too, became trapped in the ice and sank, drowning the crew. Manton and Last jumped on to an ice floe, and eventually reached the *Starry Crown,* still intact with her gold. Then, according to Last, Manton went mad and attacked his partner, who shot him in what he claimed was self-defense. Last, without the gold, managed to reach open water and was rescued by a whaler, leaving the *Starry Crown* and her precious cargo in the ice's firm grip, perhaps for ever.

Above:
Beneath its tourist's-eye delights of sky and sea, the Caribbean is perhaps the world's richest underwater treasure-store.

The 1715 plate fleet

For more than 200 years, the Spanish conquerors of the New World systematically plundered their transatlantic territories, shipping vast quantities of gold, silver, and other precious materials back to their perennially impoverished homeland. Between about 1552 and 1648, three convoys or 'plate fleets' a year made the hazardous journey from the Spanish Main. The ships were laden to the gunwales with treasure, including silver from the mines at Potosí, in what is now Bolivia.

The plate fleets were a natural target for Spain's enemies, in particular England and Holland, and for freebooting pirates owing allegiance to no nation. However, they were escorted by fighting galleons, and nine out of every ten of the ships managed to get through. Their worst enemy was the treacherous weather of the Caribbean, where shallow waters and hurricanes at certain times of the year combine to create conditions that are a deathtrap for heavily laden and cumbersome sailing vessels. Many foundered between Florida, the Bahamas, and Bermuda, their last safe anchorage in the New World.

A fortune fathoms deep

One of the biggest single disasters to befall a Spanish plate fleet occurred in July 1715, when a 12-ship convoy left Havana in Cuba carrying 6.5 million pesos (at then-current values) in gold and silver bullion and coin, and the equivalent amount in contraband smuggled aboard by the crew in defiance of the death penalty which was the punishment for such actions in Spain.

The fleet consisted of five ships from the New Spanish flota (fleet), a further six Spanish ships from Panama, and one French vessel. In addition to bullion and coin, they carried cocoa, brazilwood, vanilla, tortoiseshell, pearls, jewelry, tobacco, hides, and rare Chinese porcelain.

Six days out of Havana, in the straits of Florida, the ships were struck by a hurricane. All but the French ship sank, with the loss of more than 1,000 lives, although 1,500 people survived. The Spaniards were quick to try to retrieve their loss. Within six months they had set up a salvage camp near Sebastian in Florida, and engaged nearly 300 Indians to dive to the wrecks. Within four years, the divers were said to have recovered most of the treasure.

That satisfied the Spaniards, and the circumstances in which the plate fleet foundered were largely forgotten, to the extent

Left:
Former building contractor Kip Wagner, president of Real Eight salvage, with some of the treasure from *La Holandesa*, one of the wrecks of the Spanish plate fleet of 1715. In front of him are two trays of gold doubloons, two gold necklaces, diamond rings, a gold bar weighing several pounds and examples of Chinese porcelain. On the table behind are hundreds more gold coins in coin-collectors' envelopes.

Above:
The ultimate source of Spain's New World wealth, Amerindians wash for gold in a river-bed. These Indians, depicted in a late 16th-century engraving, are in Florida, which could not compare in its output of wealth to Mexico and Peru, further south.

that later historians disagreed over where the disaster had taken place. They proposed two sites, 200 miles apart and both wrong.
In reality, the wrecks were spread over 50 miles from Cape Canaveral to 5 miles south of Fort Pierce Inlet.

Wagner hits the jackpot

It was not until 1948, when a Florida building contractor called Kip Wagner discovered seven silver coins on the beach at Sebastian, that the treasure once again exerted its lure. Wagner worked in secret, combing the archives for references to the loss of the fleet, and observing the action of wind and waves on the Florida coastline. He reasoned that the location of the Spanish salvage base would provide the key to that of the wrecks, and found it near Sebastian with the aid of a mine-detector. His research showed that the base had been raided while the Spaniards were still trying to raise the treasure – perhaps by English freebooters.

Wagner's persistence paid off. In 1959, he partly lifted his veil of secrecy, engaging amateur divers to help pinpoint the wrecks. He

found seven or eight of them (the exact details are still wrapped in mystery), established legal title to the relics, and created a museum in which the finds could be displayed.

Prominent among them was a gold whistle on a golden chain of 2,176 links, the insignia of a Spanish fleet commander. Within the whistle, shaped as a dragon, was a solid gold toothpick, of which Wagner commented: 'What kind of dinner can a man eat to pick his teeth with that?' It has been valued at up to $60,000.

Wagner recovered Spanish pieces-of-eight – more than 1,000 in one day alone – and individual and fire-fused silver coins. There were also 28 undamaged Chinese porcelain vases and an authentic treasure chest, a wooden box 3 × 1 × 1 feet (90 × 30 × 30 cms) in size, crammed with 3,000 silver coins.

So far as is known, three or four wrecks from the 1715 plate fleet still remain to be located in the straits of Florida.

Above:
A diver works on the wreck of a
Spanish galleon off the Florida
coast. Altogether, 11 treasure-
ships foundered there in 1715 and
so far as is known at least three
of them still have to be found.

Left:
This gold chain and whistle was
part of the insignia of a Spanish
fleet commander. It is just one of
the priceless artifacts recovered
from ships of the 1715 plate fleet
lost off the Florida coast near
Sebastian.

Red gold of the Arctic

The Barents Sea, north of Norway and inside the Arctic Circle, produces some of the worst conditions faced by sailors anywhere around the globe – temperatures that can drop to 30°F below zero and tearing winds that lash the waters to a frenzy, coating superstructures with thick layers of ice and snow. In peacetime it is no place for the faint-hearted; during World War II, when the threats of enemy submarines, surface ships, and aircraft were added to the natural hazards, it was an icy hell on earth.

From 1941, when Hitler's Germany invaded the Soviet Union, the Barents Sea became a theater of war. The beleaguered Russians were desperate for weapons, aircraft, tanks, and all the other materiel of conflict from their new allies, the USA and Britain. The main supply route lay through the Barents Sea, to the ice-free northern Russian port of Murmansk, and along it steamed convoy after convoy to stiffen the Russians' resistance. In 1942 alone, some 1.7 million tons of equipment were sea-freighted to Murmansk; about 275,000 tons were lost on the way, with dozens of ships and hundreds of men.

The ill-fated Convoy QP11

The Russians paid for their armaments in nothing less than gold bullion. On 25th April 1942, the British cruiser *Edinburgh* loaded aboard 465 ingots, packed five at a time into cheap wooden cases, part of the reimbursement to the USA. The cases were described as ship's stores and stowed in the bomb-room. With her precious cargo – worth about $62 million at today's values – the ship sailed north along Kola Inlet toward the open sea, ostensibly just another escort vessel for the returning Murmansk convoy QP11. The *Edinburgh* was some 15 miles ahead of the convoy when a German submarine struck, firing three torpedoes that partially crippled her but left her afloat. She attempted to limp back to the main body of QP11, with protection from two other British warships. However, the Germans had not finished, launching three destroyers into the fray in addition to the submarines. At the culmination of a battle that lasted altogether for three days, the *Edinburgh* was again torpedoed, in the early morning of 2nd May. Still she did not sink, although heavily damaged and with 57 of her 700 men dead.

The survivors were taken off by the escort ships for the return to Murmansk. Rear-Admiral

Above:
The gallant cruiser *Edinburgh* endured three days of enemy attack and several direct hits by torpedo in the icy waters of the Barents Sea in 1942, but remained afloat. Eventually she was sunk by her own side, to prevent her cargo of gold bullion from falling into German hands. All but 34 of her gold ingots were eventually recovered in 1981, in the deepest underwater salvage operation so far completed.

Stuart Bonham-Carter, in overall charge of the convoy, then took the decision to finish off the gallant *Edinburgh* so that she and her cargo should not fall into enemy hands. At 6.30 pm, the escorting destroyer *Foresight* fired a torpedo into her hull. The *Edinburgh* rolled over and slipped beneath the icy waters, to what seemed an inaccessible grave more than 800 feet down.

Stormy salvage

There she rested undisturbed for nearly 40 years, but the lure of gold and the advance of technology meant that she was not destined to remain in peace for ever. Keith Jessop, a Yorkshireman who had wide experience as a diver both in salvage and on North Sea oil-rigs, became obsessed with the *Edinburgh*. After years of research and an abortive attempt to trace the wreck, he struck a deal with the Aberdeen diving contractors Wharton-Williams to help in raising the gold.

Matters were not simple. The *Edinburgh* had been declared a British war grave, restricting access to it. Other salvage companies were also interested in obtaining permission to dive for the wreck. And the Soviet Union, which had a partial claim on the gold, was suspicious about

Jessop's plans. Eventually, the difficulties were smoothed over, the contracts signed, and the exact position of the *Edinburgh* traced by a combination of sonar and underwater video. All was set for the gold-hunt to begin in the fall of 1981.

For the recovery attempt, Wharton-Williams, who were mainly responsible for the technical side of the operation, employed a recovery vessel called the *Stephaniturm*. From this floating base, 12 divers, working in pairs and using a diving-bell, descended to the wreck. They dived from 17th September to 7th October and managed to find in the cold, murky waters 431 of the 465 ingots.

The salvage of the *Edinburgh* is probably the deepest so far carried out, and one of the most valuable. It yielded $56 million, of which about $20 million went to the Soviet Union, and about $11 million to the British government. Of the remaining $25 million, 90 percent went to Wharton-Williams and just 10 percent to Keith Jessop. The 34 bars still left on the wreck when the dive was abandoned because of poor weather are worth about $8 million − quite possibly not enough to justify the costs of retrieving them.

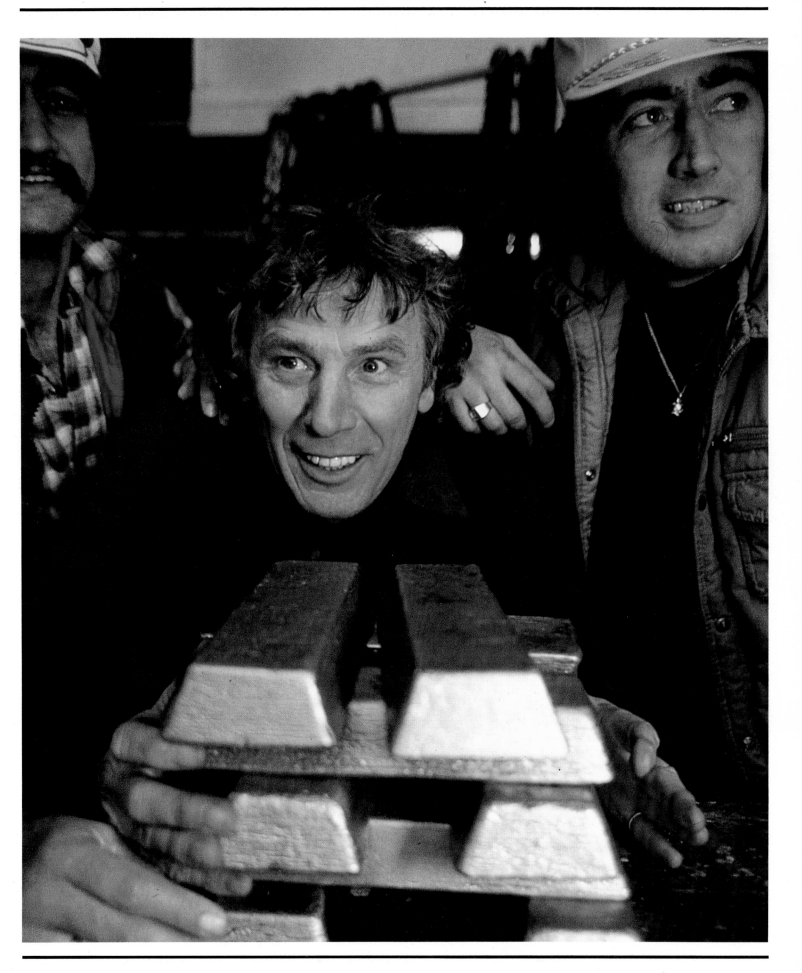

The pride of monarchs

Above:
A 16th-century manuscript now in Magdalene College, Cambridge, lists the armaments of the *Mary Rose*, pride of England's battle-fleet in the reign of King Henry VIII. Wrecked in harbor by a freak gust, she lay buried in mud until archaeologists began excavating her in 1973.

From the middle of the 15th century, Europe's maritime powers began building vast floating fortresses to support their conventional shipping in times of war. These huge vessels were not intended to stay at sea for long – generally, they never ventured more than about 24 hours' sailing from a friendly port – so they were not subject to the same constraints of design and construction that applied to smaller galleons plying the open oceans in search of new sources of wealth.

The monarchs of Europe vied with each other in building such leviathans. In 1418, Henry V of England's pride was the *Grace Dieu,* which displaced 1,400 tons (until around 1600, the biggest galleons were no more than 600 tons). Henry VIII's *Harry Grace à Dieu* was 1,000 tons. The vessels were cumbersome enough because of their weight, and their fitters made matters worse by cramming them with as much cannon as possible to create intimidating fire-power.

Unfortunately for those who manned such ships, this left them top-heavy and vulnerable in all but the calmest conditions. Several sank in weather that would hardly trouble conventional galleons – among them, England's *Mary Rose* and the Swedish *Wasa,* the objects of two of the most remarkable underwater salvage operations of recent times.

The fall and rise of the *Mary Rose*

The *Mary Rose* was relatively light for a floating fortress, just 600 tons. But she had been originally designed as a conventional warship, and then enlarged and refitted to carry 60 guns. To accommodate the cannon, gun-ports had been cut into the sides of the hull – an innovation in the mid-16th century.

On 18th June 1545, the *Mary Rose* was riding at anchor in Portsmouth harbor with the rest of the English fleet, waiting to do battle with the French. Suddenly, as the result of a breeze, she heeled over and, to the horror of the onlookers, who included Henry VIII, sank, drowning all but about 50 of the 700 men on board. The gun-ports had been left open, and the water rushing through those probably contributed to the swiftness of the disaster.

For more than 400 years, the *Mary Rose* lay at the bottom of Portsmouth harbor, until she was relocated under 15 feet of mud by divers in 1965. From 1973 onward, archaeologists worked on the wreck, eventually raising a substantial portion of the timber hull. As a fighting ship, the *Mary Rose* was not carrying treasure of the conventional kind, but she yielded a vast array of artifacts – including weapons, musical instruments, and the personal possessions of crew members, some of which are unique.

The fate of the *Wasa*

If the loss of the *Mary Rose* was a humiliation to Henry VIII, that of the *Wasa* was an even bigger one to King Gustavus II of Sweden. In the 1620s, the Swedes knew little about building large warships, so they hired a Dutchman to design one for them. The result was a square-rigger 180 feet long with a displacement of 1,400 tons and two continuous gun-decks with ports, carrying cannon weighing a total of 71 tons. As befitted the pride of the Swedish navy, she had an elaborately carved and sculptured superstructure reminiscent of a castle. That, and the cannon, gave her a dangerously high center of gravity.

In August 1628, the *Wasa* set off on her maiden voyage. But she had hardly left her moorings when she, like the *Mary Rose,* was caught by a sudden gust of wind. She immediately heeled over and sank, off the island of Beckholmen in Stockholm, at the approaches to the open waters of the Baltic.

The wreck was relocated in the 1950s, using a core-sampler, a device for obtaining specimens of the sea-bottom for analysis. The *Wasa* was raised in 1959. The timbers were in a remarkably good state of preservation, because destructive creatures such as ship-worms are not very active in cold northern waters. The artifacts too, were in good condition, including cannon, coins, cooking pots, and clothing belonging to the crew.

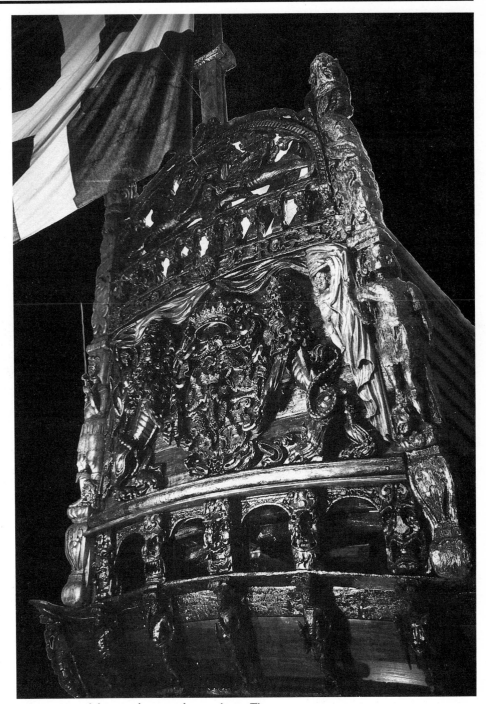

Above:
The restored hull of the Swedish warship *Wasa* has a lavishly carved and sculptured stern featuring the Swedish royal coat-of-arms. This floating palace capsized on her maiden voyage in 1628 and was raised in 1959.

Death of a battle fleet

Above:
The English fleet that challenged the might of the Spanish Armada had fewer ships and men than the enemy – but nearly twice the number of cannon. Daring seamanship by English captains such as Drake, Hawkins and Frobisher left the Spanish outmaneuvered, and fireships broke up the Armada's close formation. Even so, only about 25 Spanish ships were lost during the engagement; as many again perished trying to round the western coast of the British Isles.

The Spanish Armada, the vanguard of Philip II's attempt to crush England in 1588, was the mightiest battle fleet the world had yet seen, a massive display of sea-power consisting of 30,000 men and 1,000 cannon aboard 24 galleons, 40 armed merchantmen, and 36 smaller vessels, supported by 25 supply ships. After two weeks of running fights against the English navy, which was outnumbered though not outgunned and was led by veteran privateers such as Hawkins and Drake, the Armada was still a formidable force of more than 100 ships.

But adverse winds and the depredations of the English had left the Spaniards without the stomach to continue the battle. On 2nd August, off the coast of Scotland, their commander, the Duke of Medina Sidonia, issued his orders. The fleet was to head back to Spain, not through the English Channel where the enemy could once more attack, but round Cape Wrath in the north of Scotland and to the west of Ireland – a passage for which the captains did not have charts. This handicap would not have mattered

if all the ships had obeyed instructions and stayed well offshore. But some, desperate for food and fresh water, ventured on to the wild west Irish coast, where they were wrecked and their crews drowned or slaughtered.

Wrecks galore!
Altogether, between 20 and 25 vessels were lost in Medina's retreat, in addition to about the same number captured or sunk in the earlier fighting. The search for the wrecks, and the treasure that at least some of them carried, continues to fascinate many people. Those that have been located – though not all salvaged – are scattered over a wide area. *El Gran Grifón* went down in Stroms Hellier, off Fair Isle in the Shetlands. The *Duque de Florencia* perished in Tobermory Bay, Scotland. *La Trinidad Valencera* sank in the Bay of Kinnagoe. Off the Irish coast, the *Girona* was wrecked on the Bunboyes Rock, off Antrim. Three wrecks have been traced in Streedagh Bay in Sligo, and the *Santa María de la Rosa* foundered on Great Blasquet Island near the Dingle Peninsula. The

The tranquil waters of Tobermory Bay in Scotland reputedly conceal treasures worth anything up to $100 million — the main pay-chest of the Spanish Armada. It was aboard a galleon variously called the *Duque di Florencia*, the *Florida* or the *San Francisco*, which sank in the bay after the Armada's defeat in 1588. Some say the vessel was blown up by a Scottish prisoner taken by the crew following an argument with local clansmen over payment for food and water. Others maintain it was sunk by the spell of a local witch, Gromshuil Mhor of Lochaber. The site has drawn treasure-seekers since 1640; later in the 17th century, the Duke of Argyll brought a diving-bell from Sweden to try to trace the wreck. Learning of the attempts and eager to claim the gold for himself, King Charles II sent a warship to stop the operation. The Duke took the matter to court and won sole rights of salvage, which his successors still maintain. But the most impressive relic so far found is a bronze cannon, attributed to the Italian sculptor Benvenuto Cellini.

San Pedro Mayor successfully rounded Scotland and Ireland, only to be blown ashore near Hope Cove in Devon. So it is possible that further Armada ships may lie almost anywhere on the western coasts of the British Isles.

Treasure: lost and found

Rumors of treasure carried by the Armada began to grow even before the fleet was finally defeated. They were fed by a prize taken by Francis Drake. In the midst of battle, Drake took time off to escort the Spanish galleon *Nuestra Señora del Rosario* ashore in Dorset, and to help himself to the 55,000 ducats she was carrying. Legends of Spanish treasure abound on the Irish coast, and it is possible that local inhabitants pillaged the more accessible wrecks as soon as they were able.

The diver Archibald Miller worked on the *Florencia* in the 17th century, but it was not until the 1960s that full-scale attempts began at salvaging the remnants of the Armada. The Belgian Robert Sténuit searched for the *Girona* off Antrim in northeastern Ireland.

In 1967, Sténuit found the site, retrieving pieces-of-eight, an anchor, and a gold chain. The following year, he returned with better equipment, and discovered a whole collection of magnificent items, now on display in the Ulster Museum in Belfast. Among them were more than 400 gold coins, some 800 silver coins and precious jewelry set with gems, including a brooch depicting a salamander, and a gold box in which holy relics were carried.

The *Girona* finds are not necessarily typical. The ship, which was Italian even though it sailed with the Armada, had taken aboard the valuables from two other wrecked vessels before foundering herself. Nevertheless, contemporary records show that the Armada was a floating treasure-store as well as a battle fleet. The prospects of such riches are more than enough to keep the quest for the Armada wrecks alive. However, even when a ship is located, disappointment may follow. The *Santa María de la Rosa,* found in 1968, yielded only two pewter plates, a medallion, and a handful of gold and silver coins.

Wreck ahoy

Above:

A British Navy salvage team looks back at the Gilstone Rocks off the Scilly Isles, where the treasure-laden ship *Association* came to grief in 1707. The wreck lies about 60 feet down, between the inner and outer rocks, in an area where dozens of vessels have gone to their doom.

Far right:

Two gold coins are part of treasure worth around $1 million salvaged from the *Association*. Nearly twice as much remains untraced; it may have been pillaged years ago by the inhabitants of the Scillies, or more recently by unlicensed divers. Or it may still be on the seabed.

Storms, winds, rip tides, rocks, and enemy vessels have been perils of the sea since man first took to the waters more than 9,000 years ago. But of all the dangers threatening seafarers until the 19th century, none was more feared and loathed than the wreckers – men and women living in coastal villages who supplemented their incomes by deliberately luring passing ships to disaster and plundering them.

The south and east coasts of Britain, from Cape Cornwall to Cape Wrath in the north of Scotland, was a notorious wreckers' haven in the 18th century. So was the west coast of Ireland, where the populations of entire villages conspired to defy the law and ransack foundered ships. Across the Atlantic, Nova Scotians and New Englanders practiced wrecking, inspiring one of the most enduring legends of the sea, that of the *Palatine*. The vessel was said to have been lured onto the rocks on the west coast of Block Island, off Rhode Island, by wreckers' lanterns on the night of 27th December 1738, and set ablaze after its cargo had been pillaged.

At their most harmless, wreckers were simply beachcombers, benefiting, albeit in macabre fashion, from the misfortunes befalling ships off

the shores where they lived. But many took an active part in shaping events, dousing or moving warning lights, or indulging in the practice called 'jibber the kibber' or 'Judas lights', in which lanterns were hung at night from the necks of grazing animals to confuse unwary navigators.

Among the wreckers' most notorious feats was the ransacking of the tea-clipper *Gossamer,* off Chivelstone in Devon, England, in December 1868. On passage to Adelaide, she was beset by bad weather in the English Channel and, handicapped by a pilot who was later found to be drunk, sailed too close to the coast and broke up on the rocks. Before the police and militia could arrive, local wreckers had stripped her of most of her cargo.

The wreck of the *Association*

Wreckers played a grisly role, too, in the loss of the *Association* and four other ships of the British Mediterranean fleet off the Isles of Scilly in October 1707. The fleet, under the command of Admiral Sir Cloudesley Shovell, was carrying $3 million in bullion and silver, mostly the property of Portuguese merchants sending it to England for safekeeping. Despite the warning of a seaman who was hanged from the mast for

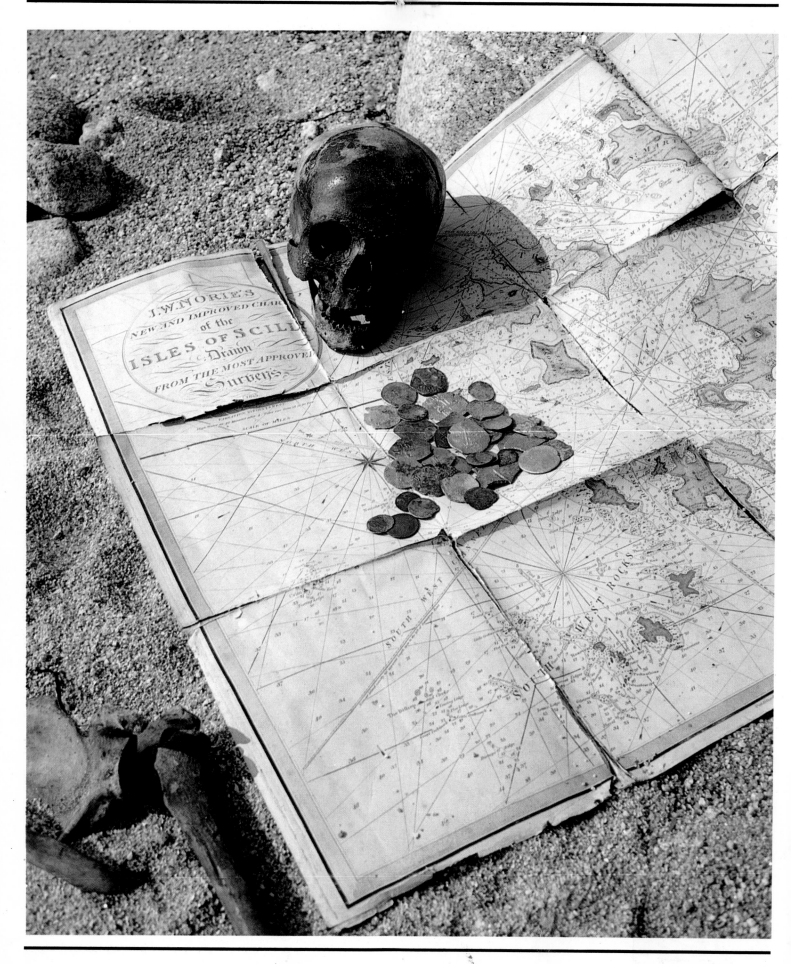

insubordination, Shovell believed he was close to Brittany, rather than over the Outer Gilstone Rock in an area where many other vessels had been wrecked. All five vessels foundered, with the loss of some 2,000 lives. Shovell himself is believed to have reached the beach alive, but to have been strangled or suffocated by local women eager to steal his personal jewelry.

The subsequent history of the *Association* is a tale of mystery and bureaucratic bungling. In a map dating from 1740, the reef on which the ship was wrecked is referred to as Shovell Rock, but the name was later changed, perhaps by locals anxious to obscure the exact location and to plunder the treasure for themselves. Alternatively, the powerful Godolphin family, lords of the Isles of Scilly from 1571, may have ordered the name-change and suppressed evidence so they could loot the wrecks and avoid having to hand the contents over to the British crown.

A salvage free-for-all

In 1967, a diving team from the Royal Navy – titular owners of the *Association* and its cargo – relocated the wreck. But underwater recovery was still in its infancy, and few ground rules had been laid down for the way in which it was carried out. The find, which included gold and silver coins and bronze cannon, was widely publicized from the first, and two other teams, in addition to the Royal Navy, were in possession of valid licences to dive to the wreck.

Other treasure-hunters were less scrupulous about the rules, with the result that at one stage there were no fewer than five teams salvaging the *Association,* together with a shifting population of freelance divers who switched allegiance from one group to another, or foraged on their own account. Few bothered to declare their finds, knowing that if they did so the British crown would claim at least half of the value. One educated estimate puts the treasure recovered at nearly $1 million, or about one-third of the original cargo, most of it finding its way into private hands. That implies that a further $2 million may still lie in the vicinity of the Gilstone Rock. But no one knows how much may have been retrieved secretly by the wreckers of Scilly over the past 250 years, either on their own behalf or acting for their masters, the Godolphins.

Far left:
A skull from the *Association* is a grim reminder of the perils of the sea — not only wind and waves, but the activities of pirates, wreckers and other cut-throats. These and many other items were raised from the *Association* in 1967.

Below:
This dramatic seascape by P.J. de Loutherberg (1740-1812) shows that victims of a shipwreck had more to contend with than simply getting ashore safely. Wreckers do battle with the survivors as they beach their lifeboat, to remove witnesses of the crime and to rob them of their personal belongings. The picture is in Southampton Art Gallery, England.

Raise the *Titanic*

No shipwreck of modern times has so captured the popular imagination as that of the *Titanic,* the allegedly unsinkable pride of the White Star Line of Liverpool, England. Holed by an iceberg on the night of 14th-15th April 1912, on her maiden voyage, the luxurious, 52,310-ton liner foundered in 13,000 feet of water some 560 miles off Cape Race, Newfoundland, with the loss of 1,513 lives. Among those who perished were no fewer than 10 American millionaires, including John Jacob Astor and Benjamin Guggenheim.

For decades, finding and raising the *Titanic* has been the dream of treasure-hunters the world over. In the late summer of 1985, part of the dream came true. A joint French-American team of scientists experimenting with underwater surveying equipment pinpointed and filmed the wreck. Their achievement immediately unleashed controversy – between those who believed the liner should be left undisturbed as a marine grave and those who argued that she should be raised; and between those who maintained that the feat of salvaging the ship from the depths of the North Atlantic was technically possible, and those who contended it was not.

Salvage claims

One of the scientists associated with the original discovery, Robert Ballard, was in no doubt. He declared that any attempt at salvage would be 'ridiculous'. But Robert Marx, a leading treasure salvager, felt the task could be partially accomplished by using robots and explosives, while conceding it resembled 'Mission Impossible'. He pointed out, 'No one has ever found anything that deep.'

At the same time, another salvager, John Pierce, won a legal victory in the British High Court which, he asserted, made raising the *Titanic,* at an estimated cost of up to $4 billion, a viable proposition. The court ruled that Pierce and his colleagues were entitled to keep items salvaged from the liner *Lusitania,* torpedoed in 1915. Pierce maintained that the decision implied that the *Titanic* and her contents belonged to whoever managed to salvage them, rather than to the successors of the White Star Line or to the insurers who had paid out on the original loss. But many English legal experts questioned Pierce's reasoning.

Above:
A contemporary reconstruction of the sinking of the *Titanic* shows several ships close to her in the iceberg-strewn waters off Cape Race. One not depicted is the *Californian,* which experts now believe was well placed to rescue many of the 1,513 people drowned. The *Californian's* behavior was later investigated, and her captain criticized for poor navigation and seamanship.

Top right:
The mighty *Titanic* undergoing sea-trials in Belfast Lough, after completion at the Northern Ireland shipyard of Harland & Wolff and before her ill-fated maiden voyage from Southampton in 1912. The hull and fixtures were insured for £1 million, a phenomenal sum at the time, and the risk spread among some 70 insurance companies and Lloyd's of London syndicates. In theory, the heirs and successors of all these insurers may have a claim on the wreck.

Below:
Shocked office-workers in London learn that the unthinkable has happened and the unsinkable has sunk in April 1912. The unique double hull of the *Titanic* was thought to give her all the protection needed against the treacherous North Atlantic.

Lost fortune

Another controversy is over the valuables that the *Titanic*'s predominantly wealthy passengers were reputedly carrying with them when the vessel sank. Some people believe that a fortune in jewelry awaits the first salvagers to reach the wreck, and that one victim – a diamond merchant – had deposited uncut stones to the value of $7 million in the ship's vault.

Most experts discount such stories, but their reasons for doing so conflict, leaving optimistic treasure-hunters with a glimmer of hope. One school of thought holds that wealthy voyagers like the Astors and the Guggenheims did not take their real jewelry with them, but traveled with paste imitations. Another cites the ship's manifest of items lodged with the purser for safekeeping; that amounted to no more than half a page, with no single item valued at more than $500 or so. The highest insurance claim lodged after the disaster was for $174,000 by a female passenger who had lost most of her wardrobe. And, said witnesses to the event, first-class travelers collected their easily portable possessions before the liner finally went down.

Two valuable items are, however, known to have been on the *Titanic* – a painting by Blondel called 'La Circasienne au Bain', valued in 1912 at $100,000, and a luxuriously bound and illustrated copy of the *Rubaiyat,* by Omar Khayyam. More than 70 years' submersion in the cold waters of the Atlantic is hardly likely to have improved either of them.

Salvager Robert Marx believes that the stories of fabulous collections of jewelry are largely irrelevant. 'Each tea cup is going to be worth a fortune,' he says. Citing the $1,000 or so now paid for a periscope lens from a German U-boat, he says a life-preserver from the *Titanic* would be worth 'whatever the market would bear' – a truism indeed!

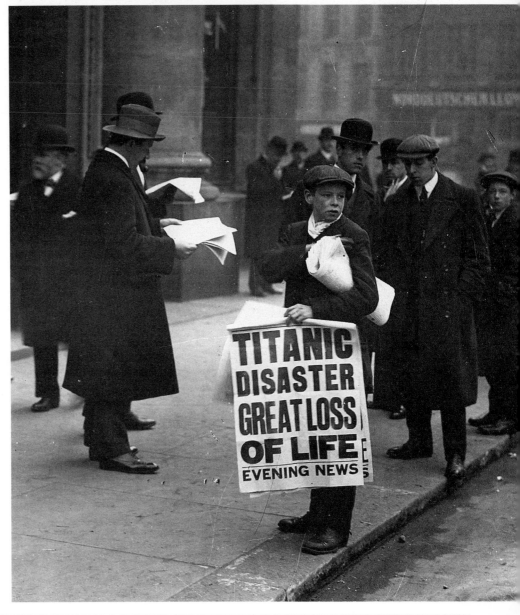

One of more than 12,000 underwater photographs taken of the wreck of the *Titanic* when she was located in September 1985 shows the bow from above, with capstans, winches and the anchor chains. The pictures were shot from cameras on the *Argo*, a prototype underwater robot sled intended for use in the US Navy's submarine warfare programme. The *Argo* can stay submerged for weeks on end and roam miles of the deep seabed, feeding back television pictures and other data to scientists aboard a mother-ship. The mission that traced the *Titanic* — jointly conducted by the Woods Hole Oceanographic Institution of the USA and France's Institute for Research and Exploitation of the Sea — chose to search for the vessel to demonstrate the *Argo's* ability 'to find something that no one else could find'.

Chapter 3

Riches from the Earth

If there is one theme which has been guaranteed to excite treasure hunters across the ages it is that of legendary 'lost riches': forgotten cities concealing the wealth of ancient tribes, abandoned mines rich in gold, silver, or precious stones, hidden hoards, and unclaimed caches. Usually such stories follow something of a pattern. It involves a lost explorer or sole survivor, convinced of the value of a find, yet curiously unable to retrace his steps to find it again. They are often tied to tantalizingly specific locations, with just enough verifiable fact mixed in among the legend and half-truths to make such stories seem feasible. Paradoxically, the very fact that the hidden treasures have never been found, instead of discouraging seekers, adds to their fascination.

The lure of El Dorado

Historically, the greatest, most exhaustive and yet least successful quest was the Spanish search for El Dorado. When the conquistadores arrived in the New World in the 16th century, they came with a cross in one hand and a sword in the other. They encountered remarkable native cultures quite outside the European experience, yet they were interested not in the least.

Within scarcely half a century, they destroyed three ancient cultures – the Aztecs, the Maya, and the Inca. Those who managed to survive the sword were caught by European disease. Ancient religions were rooted out and persecuted, cultural practices erased. All the Spaniards wanted was loot, and that they took

in prodigious quantities. So much so that they were reluctant to believe that their supply was depleted by the first hauls – although Atahualpa's golden ransom can scarcely have left much in the Inca treasury. They became convinced that there was more, and still more, to be found. Much, they believed, was deliberately hidden from them. And when they had tracked down and ransacked that, they began to listen to rumors of fabulously wealthy people living just beyond their reach. So began the quest for El Dorado, that mirage conjured from gold-fevered brains. Expedition after expedition sought it, many men losing their lives in the process, for El Dorado was never more than a myth.

And yet, in time, the image of Inca gold, or Aztec gold, became mixed up with lost Spanish gold, until the whole American continent south of Arizona and Texas became a possible source of lost treasure belonging to someone or other. It's interesting that many of the stories of lost treasure from the southern United States include a reference to long-dead Spaniards. They have continued to fascinate, through the 19th century up to the present day. Just occasionally, dramatic archaeological or historical finds turn up to give them credibility. The fantastic stories of cities buried beneath the jungles of Central America led Stephens and Catherwood to the temples of the Maya in the 1840s, and Thompson to the ceremonial well at Chichén Itzá, with its priceless haul.

Colonel Fawcett's expeditions

If the Maya could be rediscovered after 300 years, might there not have been other civilizations, lost in the impenetrable rain forests of, say, Brazil? The British explorer Colonel Percy Fawcett certainly thought so. He'd heard the story of the 'Lost Mines of the Muribeca', a tale of fabulous wealth in the mountains several hundred miles from the coast of Brazil, once exploited by a Portuguese half-caste in the 17th century. In 1753 a strong Portuguese expedition had set off in search of the mines. It was away for 10 years, and returned with a detailed account of its adventures, which described finding the mines near a waterfall in a range of white crystal mountains, not far from a mysterious and deserted ancient city. Many have since tried to find the mines, some claiming a degree of success. In 1921 Fawcett set off alone to find them and after wandering through the jungle for three months, claimed to have found the lost city. He made another expedition in 1925, but was never seen again. Even today some parts of the area covered by his expeditions remain largely unmapped, and it is just possible something may one day be found there. If so, it will not be the fabled wealth of the Muribeca which will cause a sensation, but the evidence of an unknown civilization in an area long insisted by archaeologists to be without one.

Above:
The conquistadores were the greatest despoilers in history, ruthlessly sacking one country after another. This pyramid at Teotihuacán in Mexico is a dramatic memorial to a lost world sacrificed to the lust for gold.

African and American caches

It was, perhaps, inevitable that during the 19th century, that great age of discovery, many should be motivated by the desire to find legendary lost tribes, towns, and treasures. During the great European race to explore and colonize Africa, many men were drawn by tales which turned out to be pure myth. Africa, south of the Sahara, proved disappointing for those keen to find lost treasures. When Cecil Rhodes conquered Rhodesia in the 1890s, he was seeking to duplicate the successful diamond and gold discoveries at Kimberley and Johannesburg. He believed the great stone circles of the Zimbabwe ruins, and their associated gold workings, to be the Ophir of the Bible. But all Rhodesia brought him were costly wars with the native inhabitants, the Matabele (Ndebele) and Mashona, and disillusion. The ruins of Great Zimbabwe produced only a handful of treasure, and in trying to find the non-existent ancient race that they were convinced had built it, the excavators destroyed most of the evidence of the real Africans who had.

Lost mines, however, continue to hold a fascination. The most famous story concerns the Lost Dutchman, which still draws optimistic treasure-hunters to the area of Weaver's Needle in the Superstition Mountains outside Phoenix, Arizona. Yet the Lost Dutchman is just one of several similar stories about abandoned workings or hidden caches. With their dramatic stories straight out of a Western, and a geography so harsh that it's easy to believe that anything might remain hidden up an overgrown canyon, beneath a rockfall, or under a tangle of mesquite, it's hard for anyone bitten by the treasure-hunting bug to resist them.

One thing is certain; there are still more than enough tales of buried treasure to keep potential seekers enthralled for years to come. Many are probably pure myth, and will keep being sought simply because there is nothing to be found. But there is truth enough behind some to suggest that, with the aid of modern technology, some lucky and persistent adventurer will one day come across some remarkable and exciting finds.

Left:
The remarkable Aztec calendar stone, proof of the central American Indians' extraordinary astronomical knowledge. But the conquistadores were not interested in learning or art; they smashed idols and destroyed codices in an attempt to eradicate religions considered pagan and barbarian, and ornaments of precious metal were melted down to realize their hard-cash bullion values. Onward, Christian soldiers!

Left:
This 17th-century German illustration captures the Spanish dreams of the search for El Dorado; a conquistador riding a llama is laden with bags of treasure. Few expeditions were really this successful.

Schliemann's Troy

Right:
Some of the magnificent items excavated by Heinrich Schliemann at the site of Troy, and dubbed by him 'Priam's Treasure', after the city's legendary ruler at the time of the Trojan War. In fact, the treasure predated the Troy of legend by nearly a thousand years. This remarkable collection disappeared from a Berlin museum when the city was overrun by the Russians in 1945.

There is more than a little romance to the story of Troy. There is Homer's epic poem, of course: the story of the beautiful Helen, kidnapped by the Trojan Paris and rescued at the cost of a 10-year war that ended only when the Trojans were deceived by the Greeks' wooden horse. But modern Troy has its romance, too, in the story of the man who struggled to prove that Homer was dealing in fact rather than myth – who proved that Troy was a real city. That man was Heinrich Schliemann.

Schliemann was born in the village of Neubuckow, in what is now East Germany, in 1822. If we are to believe his own account – and by his own admission Schliemann was quite happy to embroider the truth to make a better story – he first became interested in Troy when given an illustrated book on the subject as a child. Certainly, by the time he had made his

fortune trading in Russia and America, Schliemann was in a position to indulge his interests, and Troy was foremost among them.

Although Homer was quite specific about the location of Troy – on the edge of the plain of the Scamander River, across from the Hellespont, or, in other words, opposite the Gallipoli peninsula in modern Turkey – most scholars considered his story mere legend. In addition, archaeology itself was in its infancy, and, when Schliemann first set out to discover Troy in 1870, he was forced to make up his techniques as he went along.

A spectacular dig
Schliemann was convinced by an English enthusiast, Frank Calvert, that Troy lay under a mound known as Hisarlik, 'the place of the fort'. Hiring an army of 80 workmen, Schliemann set

Left:
At Mycenae, Schliemann found treasure to rival that of Troy. The golden death masks, one of which Schliemann believed belonged to Agamemnon himself, are well known, but there was much more, including this beautifully wrought gold and cornelian necklace.

to with typical enthusiasm. He first drove a great trench into the north face of the Hisarlik mound. What he found astonished him, for under the surface lay a jumble of ruins up to 50 feet thick in places. Schliemann was confounded by this mass of evidence and, since modern methods of dating archaeological strata were not then known, he presumed that the ruins were the remains of later cities, and that the Troy of legend was surely the bottom layer. With characteristic energy, he plowed downwards for two years, until at last he came to a layer bearing evidence of fire and destruction. At last, he believed, he had found Homer's Troy. And he made an even more dramatic discovery. According to his diary, quite possibly rewritten at a later date, on 14th June 1873 Schliemann found gold: more than 8,000 golden objects – cups, vases, bracelets, and necklaces. He immediately concluded that this was the hoard of King Priam, Troy's legendary ruler. Schliemann draped his young Greek wife Sophia with some of the more spectacular items – 'The Jewels of Helen' – and had her pose for photographs. To the disgust of the Turkish authorities, he smuggled the jewels out of the country and took them to Berlin.

Troy and Mycenae

It is now accepted by archaeologists that Hisarlik was very likely the site of Troy, and was destroyed no less than nine times during 4,000 years of occupation. It had 47 distinct layers of habitation, from a Neolithic settlement established in 3600 BC to the Roman city of New Ilium, which declined about AD 500. Schliemann's excavations had destroyed many of the later layers, including part of Troy VI, widely held to be Homer's Troy, in his naive drive to find something deeper and older. Schliemann's treasure, in fact, dated from around 2200 BC, nearly 1,000 years before Priam. For all his misdirected enthusiasm, he had, however, confounded the classical scholars, and proved Troy *did* exist.

What of the gold items themselves? They were housed in the Ethnological Museum in Berlin until the outbreak of World War II, when they were broken up and hidden. Like many another treasure, they have not been seen since the Russians overran the city in 1945.

Fate had more delights in store for Schliemann. Flushed with his success at Troy, he traveled to Mycenae, another of Homer's heroic kingdoms. In search of the hero Agamemnon, Schliemann dug trenches inside ancient Mycenae's surviving walls and, again, in spite of classicists' scoffing, made another astonishing find. He uncovered the graves of 19 people – he immediately assumed them to be Agamemnon's family – including three men clad with breathtaking gold armor and masks. As the story has it, when he removed the mask from the most imposing of the remains, the features on the skull beneath it were still visible; transfixed, Schliemann, the romantic founding father of archaeology, is said to have cried 'I have gazed upon the face of Agamemnon!'

Above:
A superb piece of gold jewelry recovered from Mycenae, dating from 1500 BC, the date archaeologists give to the Trojan War, if it really did take place. Schliemann's desire to prove the stories of the war as fact laid the foundation for the understanding of the glories of pre-Classical Greece.

'King Solomon's mines'

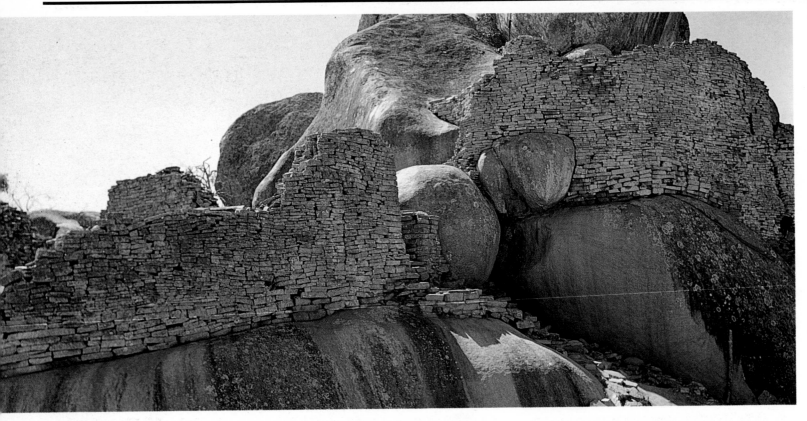

Above:
The so-called 'acropolis' of Great Zimbabwe. The superb construction of the dry-stone walling, here built to follow the contours and boulders of a natural kopje, convinced racist early explorers that the ruins could not be of African origin. In their search for proof of the mysterious lost race that they imagined had built Zimbabwe, early untrained enthusiasts destroyed most of the evidence of the real Africans who did.

Scattered across modern Zimbabwe and into Mozambique are more than 150 mysterious historic sites, the most famous of which is the ruin Great Zimbabwe, 150 miles east of the city of Bulawayo. Great Zimbabwe comprises no less than 60 acres of imposing ruins, carefully constructed, formidable drystone walls feet thick and up to 30 feet (9m) high. At the center of this complex is the so-called Elliptical Building, a great oval wall, 280 yards (256m) in circumference and containing the remains of further stone constructions.

The destruction of African artifacts
For most of the 19th century, the country of Zimbabwe itself was known only through the stories of travelers, hunters, and adventurers, some of whom brought back tales of the dramatic and deserted ruins. To visionary souls in settled South Africa, they suggested evidence of a long-vanished race of ancient splendor. Mixed up with garbled accounts of a fierce native empire nearby – the Matabele – these stories provided the novelist Rider Haggard, for one, with the inspiration for his tale of *King Solomon's Mines*. Zimbabwe was known to contain long-abandoned gold mines, and the promise of mineral wealth prompted empire-builder Cecil Rhodes to float the British South Africa (B.S.A.) Company, which in 1890 occupied Mashonaland, an area that included the Great Zimbabwe ruins.

Colonial attitudes at the time found it hard to accept that native Africans could be capable of the level of skill and motivation necessary to construct such wonders, and the first white settlers followed the prevalent line of thought that the ruins were the work of some distant superior race – the Phoenicians, perhaps, who held an almost mystical fascination for the Victorians. Rhodes himself was convinced that Great Zimbabwe was the Ophir of the Bible. In 1891 the B.S.A. Company, together with the Royal Geographical Society, sponsored an expedition to look into the origins of the ruins. It was headed by J Theodore Brent. Brent made extensive digs around the site, to a depth of several feet, but, although he uncovered many African artifacts which he dismissed as 'native rubbish', he could find disappointingly few clues as to the complex's origins. He made a stab at a date – placing construction around 1000 BC – and blandly dismissed the creators as an ancient race from the Middle East.

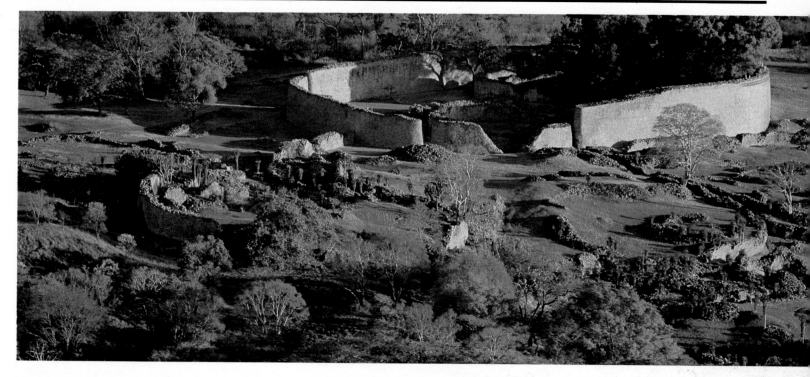

Evidence of gold workings

Brent was, at least, motivated by a desire for knowledge, but elsewhere in Rhodes' country the lure was profit. In 1893 the B.S.A. Company had gone to war with and defeated the Matabele, and the country was opened up for exploitation by the victors. A noted scout, F R Burnham, began to dig in the ruins at Dhlo Dhlo, and was rewarded by a find of 641 ounces of gold ornaments. At the Mundie Ruin, two graves were discovered revealing skeletons draped with 208 ounces of gold. Evidence of ancient gold workings was plentiful, and it was enthusiastically estimated that they must have produced, in the past, at least 21 million ounces of gold. In September 1895 the company gave the Rhodesia Ancient Ruins Ltd Company permission to dig in the historic ruins to search for treasure. Rhodes, who was fascinated by Great Zimbabwe itself, insisted that that site was not to be touched. Nonetheless, the company explored some fifty-odd ruins, turning up another 700 ounces of gold at Dhlo Dhlo, and 178 ounces from the Chumnungwa and Mtelegwa sites. Not until several years had elapsed did anyone realize the damage that was being done by these haphazard digs.

In May 1902 Richard Hall was appointed curator of the site of Great Zimbabwe. Determined to get to the bottom of the mystery, literally, Hall began excavations to find what he considered to be the level of habitation of the builders of the site. Still looking for the mysterious long-lost race, he ruthlessly cleared out the accumulations of African debris. He found a few gold items, some exotic pottery, and some beads, but of the Phoenicians there was no sign.

What such unenlightened endeavor had done, of course, was to destroy the very evidence to the site's origins that it was searching for. In 1929 the first professional archaeologists investigated the ravaged Great Zimbabwe site and concluded that it was probably medieval and undoubtedly African. The 'native rubbish' so carefully purged had been the key to understanding generations of black African habitation. Subsequent work using modern archaeological methods has confirmed that, while the many ruins were built at different times and occupied by changing peoples, all were unquestionably indigenous Africans, and the citadel of Great Zimbabwe itself was constructed scarcely earlier than 1450. A few ounces of looted gold were poor compensation for the debunking of a myth, although Great Zimbabwe can perhaps be consoled that it has given its name to the state that has replaced Cecil Rhodes' private-enterprise empire.

Above:
The extraordinary elliptical temple at the heart of the complex of stone ruins known as Great Zimbabwe. These ruins fascinated white adventurers who visited them early in the 19th century, and speculated on their origins, deciding they must have been built by some long-forgotten ancient race. The ruins were widely believed to conceal gold and gems, and Sir Henry Rider Haggard was inspired by such stories to write his bestselling adventure novel *King Solomon's Mines* (1885). In the fiction Haggard's heroes return laden with diamonds; in fact, the ruins' treasures were largely gems of archeological knowledge.

Minoan Crete

Right:
Sir Arthur Evans, pictured at an exhibition of Greek antiquities in 1936, surrounded by items from the Minoan palace at Knossos, which he excavated. On the right is a model of the Throne of Minos, legendary ruler of Knossos and keeper of the Minotaur. Minoan civilization collapsed so swiftly and thoroughly that it has been identified as a possible source of the Atlantis legend.

Below:
A modern town perches precariously on the cliffs of Santorini. The cliffs are the remains of an old volcano, whose core was blasted out in a terrific explosion that sent tidal waves and clouds of volcanic debris to overwhelm Minoan Crete, 70 miles across the sea in 1470 BC. Was this the origin of the legend of Lost Atlantis?

The legend of Atlantis, the rich island empire suddenly swallowed up by the sea in ancient times, has fascinated scholars and treasure-seekers alike for centuries. The great philosopher Plato (427-347 BC) gave the outline of the story in two of his works, and lost Atlantis has been sought across the world ever since. Many regarded it as a myth, like Homer's Troy: but with Schliemann's discoveries at Hisarlik lending substance to the Troy story, a number of amateur archaeologists were spurred to make similar discoveries, and from these have come clues which have led some to believe that Atlantis has at last been found.

Sir Arthur Evans was a British enthusiast who followed Schliemann's footsteps. He was not inspired by Schliemann's obsession with Troy but, as a scholar, was intrigued by the origins of the Bronze Age civilization that Schliemann had discovered in the Aegean. Evans's interest in early forms of writing, in particular, led him to Crete, where earlier, halfhearted excavations had revealed the existence of extensive ancient ruins. Evans bought a site known as Kephala, a low mound on the coast of northern Crete, long rumored to be the site of a great ruined palace, Knossos, and began excavating in 1899.

The legend of the Minotaur

His finds were no less spectacular than Schliemann's, for Evans, too, discovered a previously unknown civilization. Crete was remembered in the old Greek heroic poems as the home of King Minos, a wise and just ruler, cursed with the affliction of a son born half-man, half-bull – the famous Minotaur. Minos demanded tribute from mainland Greece each year, and had human sacrifices given to the Minotaur in the labyrinth. This was a palace so complex that neither monster nor victims could find their way out of its maze of corridors. According to the story, the Greek hero Theseus finally slew the Minotaur and escaped by following a thread with which he'd carefully plotted his route. Evans took the name from the legend, and named his civilization Minoan Crete. Astonishingly, echoes of the Minotaur legend abounded: the Minoans had a clear cult of bull-worship, and the remarkably preserved palace at Knossos was indeed constructed with labyrinthine complexity. There were no sensational gold death-masks, such as Schliemann found at Mycenae, but there were tons of pottery, exquisite bronze figurines, and the palace walls retained frescoes revealing the remarkably vivid and lively cultural and artistic life of the ancient Cretans. And Knossos was not alone – it was merely the dominant city of a civilization that had once covered the whole island.

The big bang

The question that continues to intrigue scholars interested in Crete is, just why did this civilization fade away, to be replaced suddenly by Greek cultures from the north? The key lies on the island of Thera (Santorini), 70 miles across the open sea to the north of Crete. Thera today consists of a circle of small islands around a deep bay, the remains of an ancient volcano which once erupted with devastating force. Indeed, there are two small active cones still smouldering in the center of the bay.

Archaeologists estimate that the Minoan civilization collapsed around 1500 BC, only the main complex at Knossos surviving to fall by conquest a generation later. And seismologists recognize that Thera blew its top about 1470 BC. The force of the eruption was incredible: thousands of tons of rock and pumice were blown out of the mountain before it collapsed in upon the magma chamber, leaving only the ring of islands and steep cliffs that remain today. Thera's steep cliffs plummet 880 feet to the bay, where the water is so deep that ships cannot anchor. They are carpeted with layers of volcanic pumice up to 200 feet thick in places. There are no contemporary accounts of the explosion, but there are modern counterparts, most noticeably the eruption of Krakatoa, Java, in 1883. The devastation wrought by Krakatoa was horrific, with up to 300 towns and villages on the Sumatran and Javan mainlands, 50 miles away, being washed away by tidal waves, and more than 36,380 people losing their lives. Tidal waves were recorded as high as 120 feet and the sun was blotted out by the volcanic cloud for hundreds of miles. And the evidence suggests that Thera, if anything, was an even larger explosion than Krakatoa.

Could an eruption on Thera have been responsible for the overnight collapse of the Minoans? Certainly, the bulk of the Minoan palaces were on the exposed northern coasts of Crete. In 1966, south of Akrotiri village on Thera itself, archaeologists discovered a fine Minoan colony, completely buried in volcanic pumice. Some of the palaces on Crete reveal ample evidence of volcanic fallout, and they were fatally exposed to the risk of tidal waves. Only Knossos, the one palace to survive, was situated on high ground a safe distance from the sea. And, in the image of a great island culture, which was suddenly swallowed up in one night of earthquake, fire, and flood, surely we find all the staple ingredients of the later Greek story – 'Lost Atlantis'.

Below left:
The civilization of the Minoan Cretans predated that of Classical Greece, and possessed a remarkably exuberant artistic and cultural life. The lively murals discovered and restored by Evans at the palace at Knossos, one of the very few Minoan centers to escape the sudden and mysterious destruction, are a true artistic treasure.

Below:
A huge storage jar from the Minoan palace at Knossos. Many such jars have been found at other Minoan sites, often cracked or broken by the heat of a smothering layer of volcano tephra, evidence of the cataclysmic eruption that is thought to have destroyed the Minoan civilization.

Lost cities of the Incas

Above:
The conquistadores of the 16th century saw value only in the bullion and precious stones from the Indian cultures they plundered, but today untold damage is done to historic sites by thieves who hack out stone carvings, highly prized on the black market for their artistic and cultural value. This elaborately incised stele from 1000 BC gives a good impression of what attracts the modern plunderers who follow in Pizarro's footsteps.

When the conquistador Francisco Pizarro entered the empire of the Inca in September 1532, he had with him a tiny army of just 130 infantry and 40 cavalry, and yet within a few years he was to devastate Inca lands and plunder one of the greatest treasure houses in history. For, although they were a highly disciplined people with a strong army, the Inca empire completely underestimated the ruthlessness and thorough brutality of the invaders. When the Inca himself, Atahualpa, Emperor and Child of the Sun God, visited Pizarro in November 1532, the Spaniards launched an unprovoked attack which slaughtered many of Atahualpa's followers and made the Inca prisoner. When he noticed, contemptuously, that all the conquistadores seemed to be after was gold, Atahualpa offered to fill a room 22 feet long by 17 feet wide to a height of eight feet with gold, and twice more with silver, in return for his freedom.

For six months Inca messengers scoured the country, collecting their nation's wealth, most of it beautifully worked offerings to the gods. But Pizarro had no finer feelings towards art, and, in one of the greatest acts of vandalism of all time, had the whole lot melted down. It produced some 11 tons of gold and 26,000 pounds of silver, a breathtaking haul by contemporary standards, and estimated to be worth over $200

million at today's prices. Atahualpa fulfilled his promise, but Pizarro broke his, and had the Inca killed anyway. He then marched on Cuzco, the Inca capital. Brushing aside all opposition, he occupied it and began systematically looting temples and treasure houses. From Cuzco alone he took items reduced to 2½ tons of gold and 51½ tons of silver. Pizarro installed a puppet ruler, Manco, in Atahualpa's place, and for two years the invaders methodically stripped the Inca lands of their remaining riches.

Manco defies the Spaniards
But the Spanish outrages grew too much even for Manco, and in May 1536 he led a revolt that trapped the Spaniards in Cuzco and came within an ace of destroying them. Pizarro, however, managed to rally his forces, counterattacked and held out until reinforcements arrived. Manco was pushed onto the defensive and began to retreat into the mountain reaches northwest of Cuzco. He built a new city at Vitcos; but when a Spanish punitive expedition located it, he abandoned it, and established himself at Vilcabamba. This was an area so remote, cut off by mountain ranges and rain forests, that he was able to use it as a safe base from which to wage a guerrilla war for several years. Not until June 1572, when Manco himself was dead and Spanish rule

Above:
A beautiful Chimu ornament from the Peru coast, vivid surviving proof of the highly developed culture of the Incas and the Indian peoples who preceded them. Of no interest whatever to the philistine Spaniards, such pots today are highly valued.

Left:
A beautiful gold mask from Peru; very little such work survives, because the conquistadores melted down Atahualpa's ransom, and whatever else they looted, for its bullion. The hope that such items might still survive among Inca ruins in remote areas continues to interest treasure-seekers in legends of lost Inca cities.

Top far left:
The mighty Inca fortress of Sucsayhuaman. From here in 1536 Manco Inca Yupanqui launched his revolt on the Spaniards in nearby Cuzco. He was nearly successful, but the conquistadores rallied, and Manco was forced to retreat further and further into the impenetrable Andes. He built a number of mountain refuges – the last, Vilcabamba, the 'Lost City of the Incas', has still to be properly explored. Although stories of forgotten treasures persist, it is unlikely that Manco's hard-pressed and impoverished followers left anything of value behind them.

throughout the rest of Inca lands established, did a column finally reach and occupy Vilcabamba. The last of the Inca's subjects, retreating before the Spaniards, had carried away what remained of the city's wealth and fired the buildings.

Search for the lost city
For centuries, as the jungle reclaimed Manco's last refuges, the legend of the 'lost city of the Incas' fired the imagination of travelers. In the early 19th century, several expeditions explored remote Inca ruins. In 1850, a Frenchman named Angrand openly admitted, while tearing holes in a site later identified as Choquequirau, that he was lured by rumors of 'immense treasure... buried among the ruins when the survivors of the race of the sun retired to the savage asylum'. Needless to say, he didn't find any.

A young American archaeologist, Hiram Bingham, whose motives were somewhat

purer, was rewarded in 1911 by the discovery of an overgrown city perched on a mountain top 2,000 feet above the Urubamba River, west of Cuzco. When the layers of jungle growth were cleared, it was found that the buildings and terraces were in a remarkable state of preservation.

Bingham was convinced that his site, called by the locals Machu Picchu, was the legendary lost Vilcabamba, and his identification was accepted, with some reservation, until an expedition in 1964 found a further complex hidden two days' journey farther along the Urubamba. This site is now widely believed to be the real Vilcabamba, although its inaccessibility has defied even modern archaeological methods. What's more, although it is an undoubted treasure, historically speaking, it's extremely unlikely that its fleeing inhabitants, already impoverished and on the run, or the pursuing conquistadores, left behind anything of financial value.

The search for El Dorado

The search for the legendary riches of El
Dorado must rank as one of the most famous
treasure hunts of all time. In 20 years, beginning
with Hernán Cortés' expedition to Mexico in
1519, small bands of Spanish adventurers, the
tough and ruthless conquistadores, had laid
waste to the huge native empires of the New
World – those of the Aztecs and the Incas. The
riches won from such sorties staggered even
those greedy soldiers-of-fortune, and from the
1530s expeditions began roving through
Central America and along the Andean chain in
the hope of finding further gold-rich peoples to
plunder. These first expeditions were drawn by
tales of rich tribes who always seemed to live
beyond the next mountain range, but it was not
until the 1540s that these stories began to
crystallize into the legend of El Dorado – the
fabulous 'Golden Man'.

The legend grows
Somewhere in the mountains around present-
day Bogotá, in Colombia, it was said, lived a
tribe who daily made offerings to the Sun God.
Each morning, before dawn, the chief of the
tribe would anoint his body with oil and resin,
and his attendants would cover him in finely
powdered gold dust, which would stick to him
until his whole body, from the top of his head to
the soles of his feet, glowed with this radiant
second skin. With his attendants, and watched
by crowds of his people from the shore, the
chief would sail out into the middle of a lake. As
the first rays of the sun struck him, the chief
would dive into the water, and, while his
attendants threw gold items in after him as
offerings, the chief would wash himself clean.
The legend of a land so rich that it could afford
such extravagant rituals, together with the
image of a lake full of priceless treasures waiting
to be recovered, came to obsess the Spanish
captains in the New World. And the story grew
with the telling. El Dorado became a place, not
a man, where all the inhabitants wore nothing
but powdered gold, and which boasted not one
but two cities built entirely of gold.

Rival expeditions set out across the Andes,
some heading northeastwards, through
Colombia to Venezuela, others descending into
the great basin of the Amazon. A few did
manage to locate wealthy tribes, and returned
with some success, but many, ranging across
bleak highland plateaus, through swamps and
impenetrable rain forests, found only hostile
Indians, privation, hunger, madness, and violent

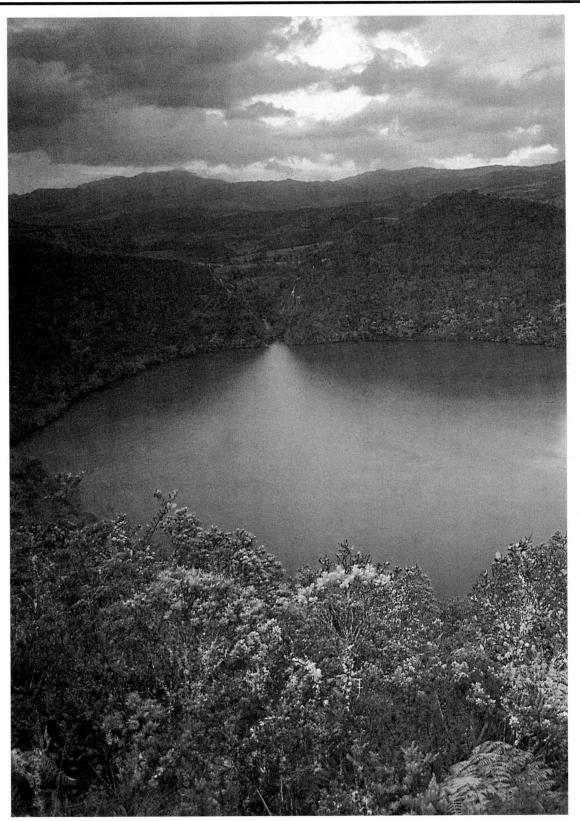

Far left:
El Dorado was not the 'golden city' of popular imagination, but in fact a fabulous 'Golden Man'. That the Colombian Indians followed a golden-man cult seems undeniable, as this superb mask and headdress bear witness, but the search for the source of the story, with its untold riches, has lured many to death and disappointment across the ages.

Left:
Lake Guatavita in Colombia, the extraordinary natural phenomenon at the heart of the El Dorado legend. Many attempts have been made to drain the brooding and mysterious lake, none of them successful, although a number of treasures have been uncovered. It remains to be seen whether modern methods, under the watchful eye of trained archaeologists, can fathom the lake's mysteries — or indeed, whether it has any secrets left to give up.

death. The rest discovered nothing but disillusion. Even the great British adventurer Sir Walter Raleigh, keen to restore lost prestige, made two expeditions. One, in 1595, explored reaches of the Orinoco; the other, in 1617, proved such an embarrassing failure that it cost him his head.

Focus on Lake Guatavita

And yet, the legend lived on. As early as 1560 the lake in the El Dorado legend was being specifically identified as Lake Guatavita, a flooded volcanic crater northeast of Bogotá. Certainly there was some circumstantial evidence to support this. The local people, the Muisca (Chibcha), were wealthy in gold when the conquistadores arrived, and did sometimes make offerings to deities thought to inhabit lakes. The first attempt to recover gold from Lake Guatavita occurred in 1562 when Antonio de Sepulveda dug a trench which drained a few feet of water from the lake, and was rewarded with '232 pesos and 10 grams of good gold'. Other attempts were made, but it was not until the 1820s that anything came of them. An enthusiast named José Ignacio 'Pepe' Paris, aided by an English naval captain, Charles Stuart Cochrane, dug several trenches and tunnels which drained considerable quantities

of water from the lake, but produced no gold. Nothing daunted, devotees estimated that the wealth hidden in Lake Guatavita must have been worth $300 million and when, in 1856, a small but beautifully wrought gold Muisca figure, depicting a chief and attendants at a ceremonial raft, was found at nearby Lake Siecha, it seemed that the El Dorado legend was confirmed.

In 1900 an English company, Contractors Limited, succeeded in draining much of the lake, although they were defeated by sludge in the deep center and by the fact that the sun soon baked exposed silt to concrete. Nonetheless they retrieved a number of gold items which were later auctioned at Sothebys in London. In 1932 an American marine diver, Jonesson, found a golden fish, death-masks, ritual vessels, pins, and pendants at the water's edge. As recently as 1965 an attempt was made to explore the lake's depths using modern diving equipment, but it was frustrated by the Colombian authorities, who were unwilling to see further amateur exploitation of an archaeological site. And so Lake Guatavita still holds a fascination for those fired by the imagined riches of its depths – despite the fact that the El Dorado legend itself has long since been discredited.

Far right:
The most popular version of the El Dorado legend has it that the Muisca Indians in present-day Colombia used to make sacrifices to the Sun God by tossing priceless treasures from a raft into the depths of a lake. The discovery of items such as this gold Muisca piece depicting a raft has not only lent credence to the story, but also given a tantilizing taste of the treasures themselves.
Below: This gold 'Sun God' mask is from Ecuador, but it is easy to see how its splendor has added luster to this greatest treasure-hunter's tale of all.

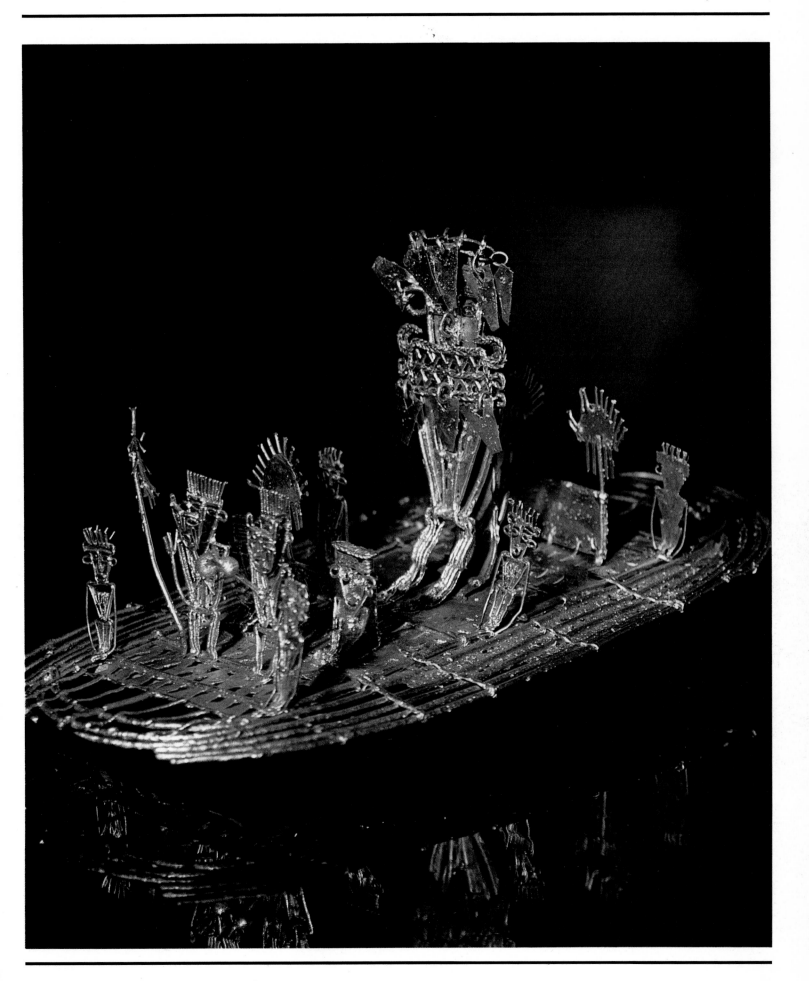

The Lost Dutchman mine

Lost mines, their location bequeathed as treasure maps by dying prospectors, are the very stuff of treasure tales, and the story of the Lost Dutchman mine has all the added ingredients of a good Western – bloodthirsty Indians, gold-lust, greed, and murder. And like a lot of classic treasure legends, the facts are so wrapped round with half-truth and myth that it's no longer possible to sift reality from rumor.

The story begins, like so many concerning gold in the Americas, with a conquistador, Antonio de Espeja, a mining engineer who wandered north through Mexico and discovered silver ore in Arizona in 1582. It is generally accepted that Jesuit miners were the first to exploit this, as they had done elsewhere, until hostile Apaches massacred them.

Gold east of Phoenix

In the mid-1800s, the family of one Enrico Peralta discovered gold somewhere in the Superstition Mountains, some 40 miles east of Phoenix. They exploited it for several years, until they too fell foul of the local Apaches. One day in 1864, the Indians ambushed the Peraltas' gold convoy, and, after a fierce three-day battle, wiped it out. A few years later, a surviving member of the Peralta family, Don Miguel, was rescued from a brawl in Sonora by two emigrant Germans, Jacob Waltz and Jacob Weiser. Impressed by their resourcefulness, Don Miguel told them the story of the mine, and offered them a share if they would accompany him into Apache country to retrieve some of the cached gold. They agreed to this, and in 1871 returned from a successful expedition some $60,000 the richer. Peralta took a 50 percent share, and presumably retired in comfort. With 25 percent each, Waltz and Weiser gradually ran out of money, and in 1879 made a return journey. They apparently found two Mexicans working the site, and had no qualms about shooting them. One day whilst Waltz was away from the camp, Weiser disappeared. Apache arrows and bloodstained clothing were evidence of his fate. Waltz left the mountains as fast as he could, but in fact Weiser had survived, and was treated by a doctor for his wounds. To this doctor he apparently told the story of the mine before he died.

Waltz, meanwhile, moved to Phoenix. In 1880 two young ex-soldiers rode into the town of Pinal one day with saddlebags full of gold. Questioned as to where they found it, they said they had stumbled on a mine by accident. It was

Left:
As the great American West was opened up in the 19th century, prospectors searched for riches in its mountains and along its rivers; these are pictured at Lee's Ferry on the Colorado River in the 1880s. For most, the reward was illusive – a hard life always at the risk of stray bandits or Indians, with nothing to show at the end of it. But just occasionally some struck it rich, and tales of their successes, such as that of the Lost Dutchman Mine, continue to intrigue treasure seekers.

Far left:
Many prospectors sought their treasure in the hills which the American Indians – this is the Arapahoe Chief Red Bear – regarded as their own sacred territory. Often the Indians reacted violently; and prospectors who discovered a priceless 'mother lode', but were killed by Indians before they could pass on its secrets, are an integral part of the Western treasure-seekers' lore.

assumed that the men had found the Lost Dutchman – archaically named for Waltz's foreign ancestry. The news soon spread, and the two men offered to return to the mine. Several days later they were found dead. They had been stripped in the Apache fashion, but had been shot with a US Army revolver. Suspicion fell on several locals, and the odd eyebrow was raised at Waltz, but nothing was proved.

A deathbed confession
In 1890, Waltz himself went back to find some gold he had hidden with Weiser. He returned with about $1,500 worth. It was his last haul, for a year later he died. On his deathbed he not only confessed to the murder of a nephew, Julius, to whom he'd told the story and then regretted it, but also described the whereabouts of the mine. Funnel-shaped, the mine was in a canyon not far from Weaver's Needle, a prominent local landmark. At least two of those who hear Waltz's last words, Dick Holmes and

Reinhart Petrash, tried to locate it, but without success.

A number of indications that mining activity once took place near Weaver's Needle have apparently been discovered, but while the mine continues to attract treasure-seekers, it has not been found. Waltz himself may have attempted to disguise it. Another story relates that the Apaches obliterated all trace of it before they were driven out of the mountains in 1885. But strange things continue to happen in the Superstition Mountains. In 1928 two deer hunters reported that someone had tried to roll rocks down on them. In 1931 66-year-old Adolph Ruth set off with what he hoped was a copy of Peralta's map. He was found dead, shot through the temple, months later, the map stolen. In 1932 two hikers were shot at by an unknown sniper. As late as 1959, a treasure-hunter named Stanley Fernandez was murdered by his partner, Benjamin Ferreira, after they quareled about sharing the workload involved in discovering the mine.

Mysterious, harsh, inhospitable, the Superstition Mountains of Arizona are the site of perhaps the greatest 'lost mine' mystery. The story of the Lost Dutchman mine is a true tale with all the ingredients of a good Western; gold, greed, marauding Indians and murder. A fortune awaits anyone who dares to defy the ominous and frequently fatal precedents associated with the mine and can find its location after more than a century.

Chapter 4

Grave Goods and Religious Treasures

Treasure associated with religions can be conveniently classified into two main kinds: grave goods interred with the dead, and biblical treasures, which may have little or no intrinsic value, but be thought of as priceless by the members of the particular faith.

The practice of burying people of rank together with their most treasured possessions was a remarkably widespread one in ancient times. People as widely isolated from each other by culture and the centuries as the Egyptians, the Celts, the Chinese, and the Amerindians all buried their important dead with valued grave goods. In each case, the theory was largely the same: the prince, emperor, or chieftain was allowed everything which might make his situation as comfortable in the afterlife as it had been in the present one. And this often included the provision of servants, too, the unfortunate retainers being sacrificed to accompany their master on his spiritual journey.

But not everyone respected the sanctity of such arrangements, even during the deceased's own times. It has been said that the first grave robbery took place a few hours after the first rich funeral, and certainly down the ages there has been a fierce struggle between those who attempted to ensure that a rich grave remained intact and those who wished to plunder it. Whatever the culture, whenever the period, few rich tombs across the world have escaped the attention of despoilers at some stage.

Pillage in Egypt

The examples of the ancient Egyptian Pharaohs are perhaps the best known. With their highly developed cult of the dead, it was essential that orthodox believers be buried with appropriate ceremony for the afterlife. We know from the tomb of Tutankhamun just what extraordinary riches went into the grave with a dead prince or king. Superb jewels, figurines, magnificent coffins – gold, gold and yet more gold. But Tutankhamun's tomb has achieved its fame precisely because it was so unusual – it was the only one of all the graves in the Valley of the Kings which had been overlooked by the grave-robbers. How tempting it must have been for ordinary Egyptians, knowing of such burials, to risk divine displeasure and severe punishment if caught for the chance of instant wealth in the here and now!

Despite the efforts of zealous priests, grave-robbing was often systematically and cynically organized by the very officials who were supposed to prevent it. It is known that many officials connived at the robbery of bodies before the tombs were sealed. Coffins have been found with built-in devices to aid robbers – disguised wooden panels which could easily be tapped out to facilitate the rifling of the body. The mummies themselves, which often had valuable charms wrapped into their bandages, were frequently simply stolen. As recently as 1985 the grave of Nephrenbet, a chief minister of Rameses II, was discovered. His sarcophagus, made of rose-colored granite, is one of the largest yet found, but when workmen

Left:
The practice of interring the dead with items of value to serve them in the afterlife was common to many people of different cultures and time spans. This remarkable museum at Dickson Mounds, Lewiston, Illinois, displays the skeletons of over two hundred American Indians, in the original positions as they were found. Buried with them were pottery, beads and artifacts of rare beauty.

Below:
The entrance to a lost world: the doorway into the King's Chamber at Ur, in the Euphrates valley, modern Iraq. When Sir Leonard Woolley explored the site in the 1920s, he discovered a remarkably complete tableau of life in this long dead civilization. King A-Bar-Gi lay in state surrounded by the bodies of his servants and dead oxen to pull his carriages.

removed the 7-ton lid they found that thieves had drilled a hole in the bottom and stolen the contents.

Early in 1986, Dr Geoffrey Martin and Dr Jacobus Van Djik, leaders of the Anglo-Dutch Exploration Society, discovered the tomb of one of the most powerful men in Egypt some 3,500 years ago. This was Maya, treasurer to Tutankhamun. Nobody knows what the tomb may contain in the way of valuables, and archaeologists estimated that it would take some three to five years to discover all its secrets. But right from the word go the experts were delighted with the miraculous condition of hieroglyphs adorning the antechamber. And what about treasure? 'We are not here treasure-hunting,' was the official reply.

All the ingenious booby traps, false passages, and other disguises built into many tombs were of no avail. It's curious, however, that few rulers seem to have resorted to the one means of protecting the dead which continues to grip 20th-century imaginations: the curse. Most Egyptian tombs simply bear inscriptions begging intruders to pray for the soul of the departed.

Early excavators
Until the birth of real archaeology in the 19th century, inquisitive individuals investigating ancient tombs across the years were little more than grave-robbers themselves. It wasn't until well into this century that proper techniques for understanding strata, the layers of soil in which items were buried, were developed, and most

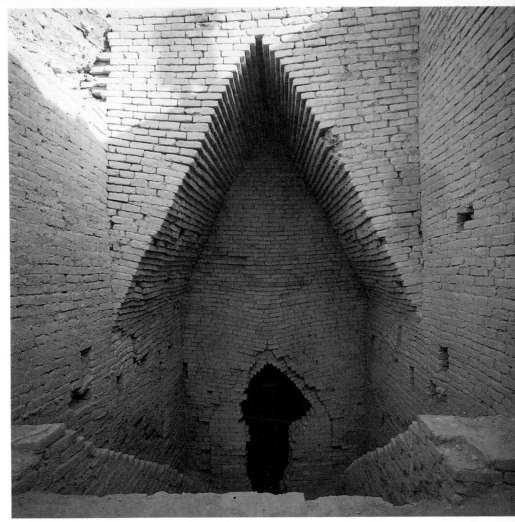

early investigators simply saw their job as being to recover whatever valuables might have been left at a particular site. They lacked the facilities to understand much else.

The first attempts to dig into the Roman cities of Herculaneum and Pompeii in the 18th century were naked treasure hunts, marked by organized gangs looting valuable statues wholesale, although later attempts were made to record what was uncovered. When in 1776 the Duke of Northumberland dug a shaft into Silbury Hill in England, his prime aim was to discover a life-sized gold equestrian statue he believed was buried there. By the end of the century, it was realized that much could be learned from such sites, but excavators were still primarily interested in removing items of value – albeit historic value, rather than strictly intrinsic.

A few of the early excavators did apply more restrained standards. No less a person than Thomas Jefferson was one of the first to be interested by evidence of old American Indian cultures. In 1784 he opened up a burial mound in Virginia. He was not looking for valuable grave goods, but simply trying to learn. With a thoroughness worthy of a modern archaeologist, he noted that the mound was clearly a tomb, for it contained a large number of skeletons, buried in layers at apparently different times. By studying the remains he came to the conclusion that the site was a civilian cemetery, not a mass war-grave as had previously been supposed, because several of the skeletons were those of women and children and none bore marks of weapons.

Historic treasures

Some sites do, occasionally, survive the ravages of the despoilers, and the modern world is allowed a breathtaking insight into the glories of years gone by. We've already mentioned Tutankhamun; the tombs of some of the Chinese emperors also have revealed breathtaking jade burial suits and artifacts. And the life-size terracotta army of Ch'in Shih Huang-Ti, far too cumbersome and valueless to tempt robbers, has been revealed to amaze us today. A 6th-century BC Celtic grave at Vix, in France, escaped the attention of thieves and was revealed to contain the tomb of a wealthy and influential woman, accompanied by her brooches, rings, armlets, a diadem of gold, a bronze statuette, and a huge bronze vessel from Greece. The least valuable of the items intrinsically, the bronze turned out to be the most interesting, because it proved the existence of hitherto unsuspected trade routes.

The practice of stripping ancient tombs is not, alas, over. Many valuable sites remain hidden to professional archaeologists, who often lack the resources to explore fully those sites they do know of. With high prices paid on the international market for examples of ancient art, the unscrupulous and cunning find ready outlets. The sites of ancient Etruscan tombs in Italy, and Anatolian ones in Turkey, are widely rumored to be plundered by professionals who keep the locations to themselves. Even communist China found it helpful to employ the expertise of known tomb-robbers when trying to excavate imperial tombs in the 1960s. And over the centuries, it is quite impossible to guess at the nature and value of the goods which have disappeared from graves around the world.

Holy treasure

Some religious treasures are sacred relics and they include the alleged pieces of the cross on which Jesus of Nazareth was crucified (although it must be said that if all the portions were gathered together in one place they would make up not one but several 'true' crosses of the correct dimensions). Relics of the saints, including clothing, possessions and even surviving parts of their bodies, have also for

Below:
One of the treasures of Ur, a golden bull's head, decorated with lapis lazuli, adorns a lyre. What survives from ancient graves is only a fraction of the original treasure, and provides no more than a tantalizing glimpse of what has been lost across the ages.

centuries been lovingly hoarded in shrines and churches around the world.

One such holy relic lies carefully guarded in the 15th-century cathedral of Turin, in Italy. It is the famous Turin Shroud, an ancient piece of cloth, which may have been the sheet in which the body of Jesus was wrapped after the Crucifixion. It is very rarely displayed for inspection, but scientific experts who have examined it have not been able to disprove the claim. The material seems to be of the correct age and appears to be bloodstained. What is more mysterious is that there is the image of a body with the outline of the bearded face clearly imprinted on the cloth. Not unnaturally, the church authorities are reluctant to allow the experts to remove portions of the shroud for definitive laboratory tests.

2,000-year-old scrolls

A multiple holy treasure, discovered as recently as 1947, was unearthed by a young Arab boy chasing a stray goat near the Dead Sea, the lake that lies between Israel and Jordan. In a cave he found some clay cylinders containing 11 scrolls. The boy and a friend sold their find to a Jerusalem dealer for a few dollars. Long afterwards, the Syrian Orthodox Monastery of St Mark paid well over $100,000 for five of the manuscripts. They have since become renowned as the Dead Sea Scrolls.

The scrolls were written in Hebrew and Aramaic, and experts have dated them between 100 BC and AD 68. Together they represent some 500 books, about 100 of which are versions of the Old Testament books of the Bible. They also describe the life and times of the community that lived in and around a monastery known as Khirbet Qumran.

In addition to providing such valuable information, the scrolls have helped to confirm biblical accuracy and historicity by bringing to light Old Testament books written some 2,000 years ago. Before this epic find, the oldest of such books in Hebrew was about half that age.

Below:
Most graves thought to contain valuables have been plundered down the ages, but occasionally one is found intact, and contains such a wealth of dazzling treasures that it becomes legendary. The tomb of Tutankhamun made even experienced archaeologist Howard Carter feel the excited anticipation of a treasure-seeker when he first peered into it. This gold statue was among the many breathtaking artifacts.

Left:
Inside the 'Palace of Virgins', a mound grave from the Macedonian empire of 250–300 BC, visitors can see a stone copy of the original wooden throne.

The treasures of the Chinese emperors

Above:
Row upon row of terracotta infantrymen, supported by chariots, a life-size army of a thousand warriors set to guard the tomb of the Chinese Emperor Ch'in Shih Huang-Ti, China's 'first Emperor' (221-210BC), the builder of the Great Wall. This is one of the most extraordinary archaeological sites in the world.

Far right:
According to Taoist beliefs, jade prevented decay of the body after death. In the case of Prince Liu Sheng and his wife Dou Wan, this proved to be a myth, for when archaeologists opened their tomb they found few human remains, but the suits themselves are of breathtaking beauty and priceless value. This is the face-mask and headcovering of the Princess.

Like the pharaohs of Egypt, the emperors of China went to their graves accompanied by a magnificent panoply to serve them well in the afterlife. And, just like the pharaohs, they were haunted by the thought that their last resting places were highly likely to be desecrated by grave-robbers. The practice of grave-robbing is as universal, and virtually as old, as the practice of burying valuables with their deceased owner. The battle between those who built tombs, and tried to ensure their protection, and those who defiled them, stretches across time to the mists of antiquity.

In China, it was the habit of emperors to build tombs as virtual underground palaces, covering them with a large burial mound, often acres in extent, and surrounded by a protecting wall. Sometimes the resulting hill was planted with trees in a naive attempt to pass it off as a natural formation. Apparent entrances were often false and, as the tomb-builders increased their skill through experience, interior passages frequently included booby traps. It was all to no avail, for the vast majority of imperial tombs in China were entered and plundered years ago. So expert were the tomb-robbers that when an

archaeological expedition sought to excavate the tomb of the Emperor Ming Wan Li near Peking in the 1960s, known professional tomb-robbers were released from prison on parole as 'special archaeological assistants'. Sure enough, they located the hidden entrance to the tomb with ease.

Tempting relics
The discovery of tombs which have survived desecration indicates that extraordinary riches could reward enterprising thieves. In 1968 a unit of the People's Liberation Army was carrying out construction work near Man-Ch'eng when they came across an artificial cave in a hillside. Archaeologists found two vast underground chambers – one 170 feet long by 121 feet wide – which proved to be the graves of Prince Liu Sheng, a member of the royal family during the Western Han Dynasty, who died in 113 BC, and his wife Dou Wan. The graves had not been plundered, and foremost among the treasures discovered were the jade suits in which the bodies had been buried. Taoist magicians believed that jade had the property of preventing the decay of a body after

death. In this case it was unsuccessful, as only a few bones remained and the suits had collapsed, but upon restoration these proved to be quite stunning. Liu Sheng's suit was some 74 inches (188cm) long, and made up of 2,498 wafers of jade, held together by 2½ pounds of gold thread. His wife's was 67¾ inches (172cm) long, with 2,160 pieces of jade, and 1¼ pounds of gold. Over 2,000 priceless bronze, pottery, and jade items were also found.

At least one grave-robber was caught in the act, and his fate left for all to see. According to legend, the young Princess Yung T'ai fell foul of her grandmother, the fearsome Empress Wu, who had both the princess and her husband put to death about AD 701. After the empress's death, the couple were re-interred by a grieving relative in a burial mound 37 feet (12m) high near Ch'ien-hsien. In 1964, when the tomb was excavated, archaeologists found a skeleton near the mouth of a tunnel dug by thieves; a trail of valuables, dropped in haste, led back to the graves.

Recent discoveries

Perhaps the most remarkable tomb was that of Ch'in Shih Huang-Ti, the 'First Emperor', a fierce autocrat who had united China by conquering warring tribes in the 3rd century BC. He is best remembered as the builder of the famous Great Wall. He was buried beneath a mound 164 feet (50m) high, Mount Lishan, in the valley of the Yellow River. Despite protective devices, such as crossbows set to be triggered by the movements of an intruder, it was widely known that the tomb had been rifled. In March 1974, however, peasants digging a well over a mile from the site uncovered some terracotta figures, which proved to be part of an army of literally thousands of life-size figures. Archaeologists patiently clearing the site believe it will be years before their work is completed, but now hope that Ch'in Shih Huang-Ti may have left his burial mound as a decoy, and that his real resting place may yet be undisturbed. If so, a treasure of legendary proportions may await the finders, for the First Emperor went to the afterlife surrounded by entire rivers made of mercury, and accompanied by a map made of precious metals.

Finds continue to be made. In 1983 the hill of Xianggan, north of Canton, was leveled, unearthing the tomb of the Emperor Wen Di. He was dressed in the traditional jade burial suit, and had been accompanied to the grave by six servants, one a woman still cradling the skeleton of a child, four concubines, and dozens of jade, silver, ivory, agate, and glass artifacts, including 43 jade ritual swords, carved with dragons and tigers.

One tomb which continues to elude the searchers, however, is that of the first Ming emperor, who ruled from 1369. The graves of 13 Ming emperors are known to exist near Peking, but the first took extraordinary measures to prevent discovery. He had no less than 13 coffins prepared for 13 tombs, and nobody knew which contained the body and its treasures when all 13 were buried with appropriate pomp and ceremony. In 1928 roadmakers uncovered a tunnel near Nanking, but it proved a false lead, and the real grave and its treasures have not yet been found.

Far right:
Enigmatic smiles distinguish the features in this delicate portrait of the ladies of the court from the Tang dynasty. The smiles hint at many mysteries about the tombs of the ancient emperors, some of which have still to be found, and which may, if the grave robbers have not ruined them, contain fabulous wealth.

Tutankhamun

'Can you see anything?'

  'Yes – wonderful things!'

With this, surely one of the most famous exchanges in archaeological history, Egyptologist Howard Carter and his patron, Lord Carnarvon, peered through a hole they had made in the sealed entrance, and became the first living persons in 33 centuries to gaze upon the tomb of the Pharaoh Tutankhamun.

Carter's discovery of the tomb was scarcely an accident, although he certainly had more than his fair share of luck. He had begun searching the Valley of the Kings, a desolate valley near Thebes in Egypt (where no less than 49 ancient rulers had been buried), in 1914, financed by his wealthy English backer, Lord Carnarvon. Many archaeologists thought that the site was exhausted and, although he found several clues which led him to believe that Tutankhamun's tomb was in the valley, Carter had had no luck in finding the tomb itself. By 1922 Carnarvon's money was beginning to run out, and only one small section of the valley remained to be explored. This was a small triangle of rock and sand at the foot of the already discovered tomb of Rameses IV.

The great discovery

Determined to have one last try, Carter ordered this patch of ground to be cleared. As he went on site on the morning of 4th November, Carter was greeted by silence from his normally noisy workmen; they had uncovered a flight of steps leading down into the ground. Hurriedly, Carter cleared the rubble, and found that the steps led to a door bearing seals in the name of Tutankhamun. With remarkable restraint, Carter then cabled Lord Carnarvon, at home in England, and waited for him to arrive. Not until the 25th was the door opened. It revealed a long passage leading to another door. Here Carter made a small hole in the upper left-hand corner, held up a candle to test for escaping gases, and then peered in.

Tutankhamun himself was not a particularly significant figure. He reigned from 1361 to 1352 BC, and had died at the age of 18, probably violently. His only real historical importance was that he succeeded Akhenaton, a heretic pharaoh who had broken with traditional Egyptian beliefs and founded his own religion. During the reign of the young and pliant Tutankhamun, the religious establishment had reasserted its power and restored the old gods. After his death, Tutankhamun had been

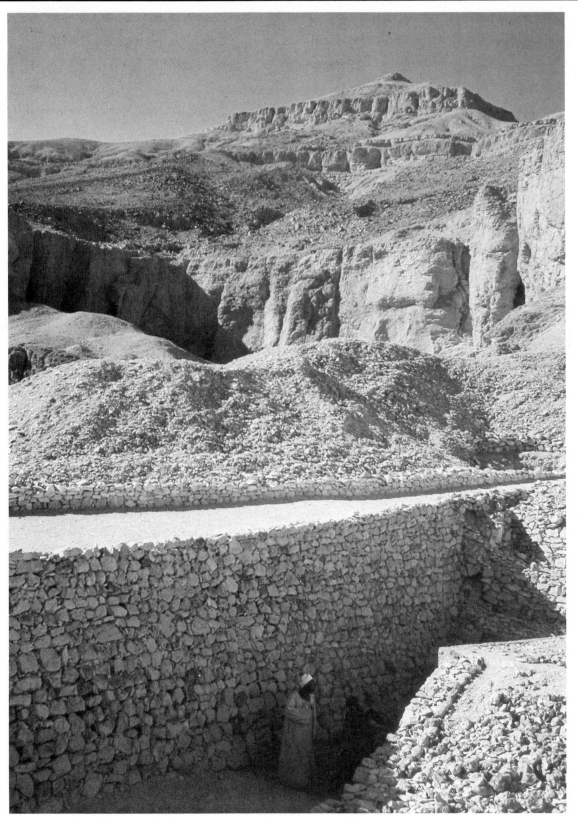

Left:
The Valley of the Kings, where
Howard Carter searched for years
for Tutankhamun's tomb.
He finally found it tucked in a
hidden corner, overshadowed by
the graves of mightier kings – but,
unlike any of the others in the
valley, Tutankhamun's had
escaped the ravages of ancient
grave robbers.

Far left:
The step pyramid of Saqqara is
older than the better known
pyramids at Gizeh, near Cairo.
The Pharaohs went to great
lengths to protect the treasures
buried in their tombs, but the
conspicuous pyramids soon
attracted the attention of grave
robbers, and few tombs escaped
plundering. The boy-king
Tutankhamun's did so precisely
because it looked so insignificant
from above ground.

Above:
Tutankhamun's throne is considered by many to be the supreme artistic treasure in the tomb. A beautifully worked and inlaid gold panel depicts the king sitting at ease, while his queen anoints his shoulder. The treasures of Tutankhamun's tomb are without parallel in the field of Egyptology.

Far right:
Breathtaking in beauty, and priceless in value, this is Tutankhamun's death mask, a lifelike effigy in gold, inlaid with obsidian and lapis lazuli, which rested on the shoulders of the body itself. Carter believed that it had captured perfectly the tranquil expression of the young king overtaken prematurely by death.

quickly forgotten. And this, ironically, was what ensured his immortality and made the discovery of his tomb so important. For, alone among all the long-dead inhabitants of the Valley of the Kings, Tutankhamun had been left largely undisturbed by grave-robbers, who had systematically plundered all the other sites, sometimes within hours of the burial. What Carter saw when his eyes became accustomed to the gloom was the full panoply of an Ancient Egyptian royal burial.

Priceless relics
The tomb itself consisted of four rooms: a large antechamber, a small annex, the sealed-off coffin-room itself, and an attendant treasure-room. With typical patience, Carter set to work cataloging, restoring, and removing the contents of each room before moving on to the next. The bone-dry conditions within the tomb had ensured that even wood and basketwork had survived the ages. In the antechamber alone there were large wooden gilded couches, life-size statues, a golden throne, and a jumble of vases, shrines, and boxes containing items for the king's comfort in the afterlife. Carter processed them all before moving on to the sepulcher. Watched by an audience of transfixed officials, Carter broke into the burial chamber on 17th February 1923. He was

greeted by a wall of gold, the outer casing of a gilded casket so large it almost filled the chamber. Tutankhamun's coffin proved a veritable Chinese box; inside the outer shrine lay another, and another, and another, and inside that a shaped granite sarcophagus. Within this lay three coffins, the first made of gilded wood, the second of wood covered with gold leaf, and the third, breathtakingly beautiful, of solid gold inlaid with precious stones and jewels. Nor was that all; when he carefully peeled away the layers of petrified funeral ointments, Carter found that the mummy itself wore a stunning gold death mask.

It took Carter five years to preserve and remove the treasures of the tomb, statues, figurines, pieces of chariots, jewels, weapons, to the Cairo Museum, and a further five to finish cataloging them. Their value was inexpressible – the inner coffin alone weighed 300 pounds, worth perhaps $250,000 just in bullion value. Yet Lord Carnarvon, whose money had made the discovery possible, did not live long to appreciate it. He died six months after the find from an infected mosquito bite, giving rise to the legend of the Pharaoh's Curse – an idea which still grips the popular imagination, despite the fact that the hieroglyphics on Tutankhamun's tomb make no mention of a curse, and the fact that Carter himself lived to be 64.

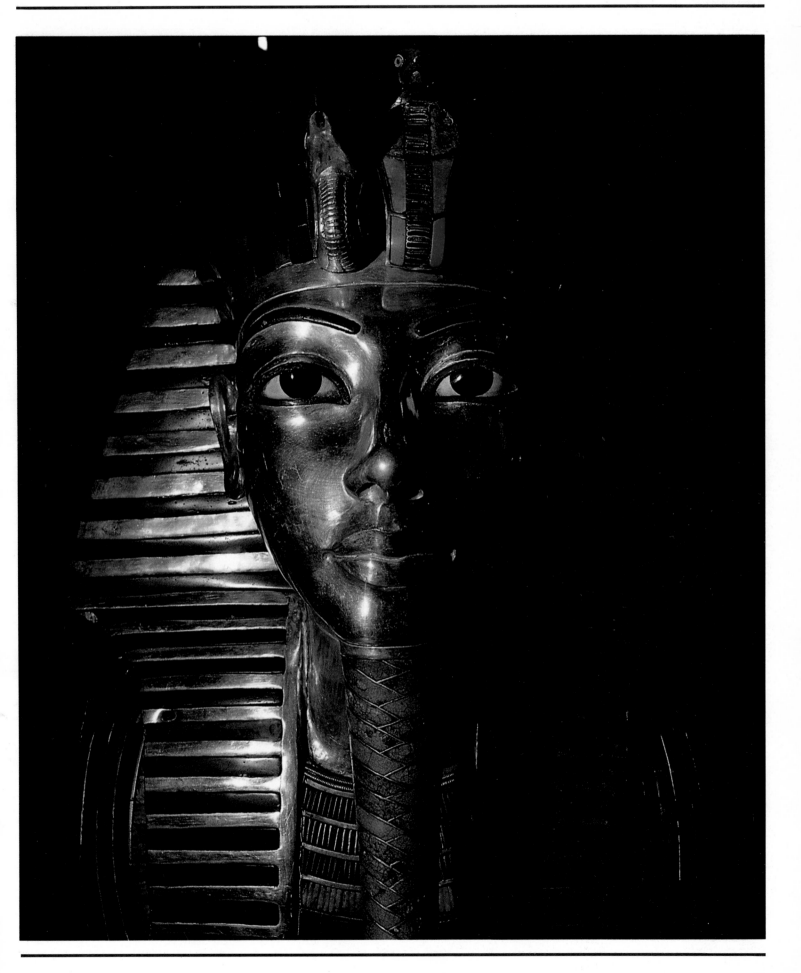

The Sutton Hoo burial

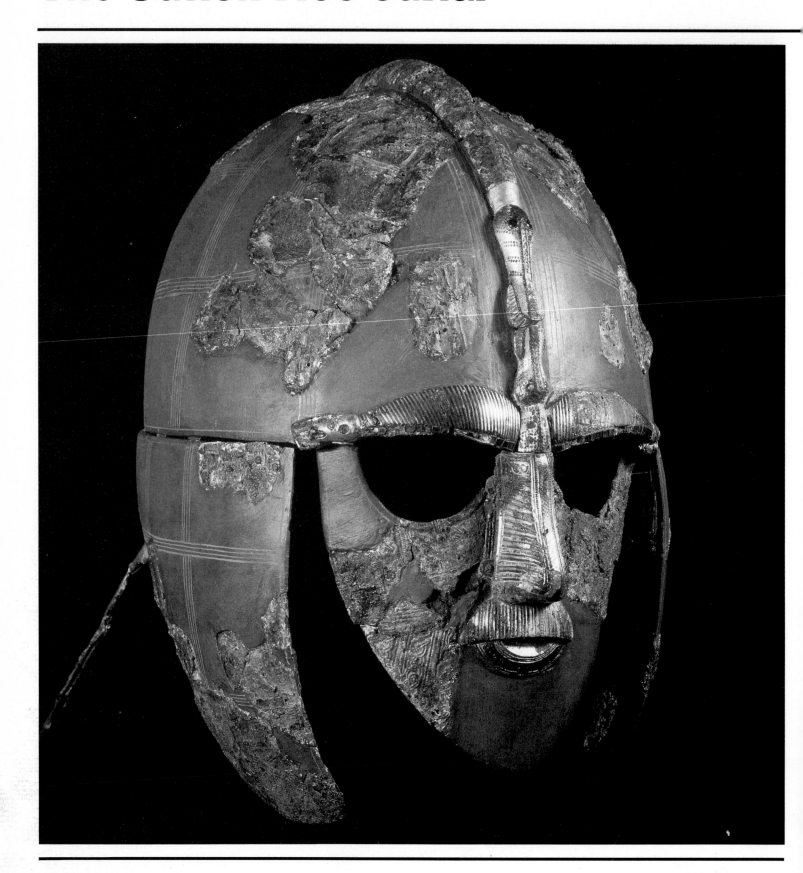

At Sutton Hoo, near the village of Woodbridge in Suffolk, England, there is a cluster of 15 or more grassed-over ancient burial mounds. Unlike many of the important archaeological sites of the Mediterranean, Middle East, or Americas, there was no great mystery about the Sutton Hoo site; its location was widely known and its purpose easily guessed. It was not until the 1930s, however, that any attempt was made to excavate the site, an enterprise rewarded by the discovery of one of the richest treasures in British archaeological history.

In 1938, the local magistrate, who owned the land on which the barrows were situated, gave permission for an amateur enthusiast to make some exploratory diggings. Several of the sites were opened, and confirmed the impression that they were burial mounds dating from the Dark Ages between the collapse of the Roman occupation and the Norman Conquest in 1066. One even contained traces of a wooden boat, suggesting that it might have been a ship-burial of a type associated with the Vikings. All the barrows had been disturbed many years before by treasure-seekers, however, and were badly damaged; the ship site, in particular, had been almost obliterated.

A ship-burial mound

The next season, in 1939, the same team turned their attention to the largest of the mounds, some nine feet (2.75m) high, without any great hopes of success. As they cut into the sandy soil, however, they came across a line of iron bolts – rivets from the planking of an ancient ship, still in their correct positions and therefore apparently undisturbed. Evidence of another ship-burial emerged and, when the team reached the center of the ship, where the body and funeral goods would have been laid to rest, they found enough items to convince them that it had escaped plundering. Since the site was clearly of the greatest importance, a team of professionals from the British Museum was called in, and a full-scale excavation began.

The results were astonishing. When the barrow was fully excavated, it was found that it had indeed covered a wooden ship, some 89 feet (27m) long. The timbers had long since rotted away, but they had left a curiously precise impression in the soil where they had been, and all the more durable items remained in place. A huge plaster-cast of the site was taken – it required six tons of plaster of Paris – and the archaeologists set to work to recover the

Far left:
Carefully reconstructed, the great iron helmet decorated with gilt is a powerful and dramatic monument to the Dark Age warrior who once wore it. Although scholars continue to speculate, his identity remains a mystery, and it is by no means certain that his body itself was interred at Sutton Hoo.

Below:
In Britain, all treasures found in the ground must be judged by an inquest to decide whether they are 'treasure trove', legally ownerless and therefore the property of the Crown, from which the finder is entitled to a percentage of the value. In August 1939 this inquest was convened to examine one of the most dramatic finds in British history – the Saxon ship-burial at Sutton Hoo, Suffolk.

artifacts. Whoever had been commemorated by the grave, he was clearly of the greatest importance, for his funeral goods were extraordinarily rich. There were great silver plates, buckled by the weight of the soil over the centuries but otherwise in excellent condition, iron goods and weapons, the silver tips and bases of great ceremonial drinking horns, and the remains of the man's personal costume. There were corroded iron fragments from a war-helmet, later reconstructed. It was a fearsome piece, with hanging cheek-guards and a face-mask that covered the whole head, decorated by beautiful gilt dragon motifs. There was the central boss of a huge shield, similarly decorated, and the remains of a sword and scabbard. Most impressive, however, were the gold buckles and clasps, decorated after the

artistic fashion of the time with robust, swirling patterns, set with garnets and picked out with colored glass. There were the fittings of a magnificent purse, still containing over thirty gold coins and small ingots.

Experts have used these to date the burial at about AD 625. In addition to these most obvious treasures, there was a no less impressive iron standard, and a stone scepter, decorated with carved faces and mounted with an iron ring bearing the device of a stag in bronze, further proof of the importance and rank of the man buried there.

Later investigations

Curiously enough, however, despite this panoply, no trace of a body was found. It was suggested that the tomb might have been more of a cenotaph, the last ceremonial rites of a leader who died in the many battles of the time, and whose body was never recovered. The outbreak of World War II prevented further examination. The treasures were removed, the hollow filled with bracken, and the site given over to the army, who used the mounds as a tank obstacle course! Years later, however, the Sutton Hoo site was reopened, found to have survived even these trials with few aftereffects, and investigated again, this time using more sophisticated scientific techniques. Sufficient traces were found in the sandy, acid soil to suggest that a body might have been present, after all, and that the skeleton had rotted away completely. His identity still remains the subject of some conjecture, however, although he was clearly a man of the greatest importance,

possibly even Raedwald, a king of the East Angles.

One thing is certain, however. The Sutton Hoo site is the most complete example of a ship-burial likely to be found, better even than the famous Scandinavian Viking examples at Gokstad and Oseberg, which, dramatic though they were, had been plundered in ages past. Sutton Hoo gives a tantalizing glimpse of the treasures that must once have been buried in them, too.

Above:
The shoulder-clasp from the cape of a king of long ago, part of the panoply that was buried with him when he was laid to rest in a wooden longship at Sutton Hoo in about 625 AD. Most of his personal ornaments were of gold set with garnets and colored glass.

Top left:
The great gold buckle from the Sutton Hoo burial. Solid gold, it weighs over 14 ounces (400 grams) and is 127mm long. It is decorated with a pattern of intertwined snakes, typical of the robust, chunky artistic styles of the early medieval period.

Albion's treasures

The British Isles are littered with the physical evidence of a dramatic past that stretches back beyond recorded history. Standing stones, grassed-over burial mounds, ancient hill-forts are scattered over the countryside and, since the gradual spread of learning awakened an interest in antiquities, all have evoked wonder and conjecture. The world-famous circles of standing stones at Stonehenge and Avebury led to a fascination with that mysterious race, the Druids of pre-Roman times. In the 18th and 19th centuries it was fashionable to attribute almost all prehistoric sites to the influence of the Druids, and, although this view is no longer held, the Druids have inscribed a dark and intriguing page at the beginning of the nation's history. Before the birth of serious archaeology, when the distinction between fact and legend was less clear, more than one enthusiast was prompted to search for treasures of the past that are now thought to be no more than mythical.

Digging for myths

In 1776, for example, the Duke of Northumberland attempted an excavation of Silbury Hill in Wiltshire, at 130 feet (40m) high one of the largest and most mysterious manmade hills in Europe. The Duke imported skilled tin miners from Cornwall, who dug an eight-foot (2.5m) square shaft from the top of the hill right down to the original ground level below. What he hoped to find was a life-size statue of one King Zel, on his horse, crafted in solid gold. Since King Zel seems to have been entirely mythical, it's not surprising that he found nothing – nor, indeed, did a rather more learned excavation in the 1960s, and the purpose of the Silbury mound remains a mystery.

Another character from Britain's legendary past who continues to attract attention is King Arthur. Numerous castles, hills, dark crags, and lakes retain legends associating them with the golden age of Arthur and his Round Table, but in this case there does seem to be a slender historical justification. Arthur was not the medieval paragon of legend, but a warlord in the Dark Ages following the collapse of the Roman presence in Britain. His Camelot was not a stone palace of glittering towers, but in all probability a hilltop refuge of palisades and trenches. Cadbury Castle in Somerset is currently held to be the most likely contender.

Far right:
Brooding and mysterious, the standing stones of Stonehenge on Salisbury Plain, England, aptly symbolize the grandeur of Britain's past. The great stone circles, one within another, are dated about 2123-1573 BC and even now their origin and function are unknown. Many prehistoric sites are scattered throughout the country, few as dramatic but many as enigmatic. Some have been excavated to reveal burial chambers, others have no apparent purpose and were regarded as haunts of old gods, and many were believed to contain legendary treasures.

Boudica, the Iron Lady

One famous story which might just bear archaeological fruit one day concerns the famous British warrior queen, Boudica, who, as Boadicea, has been romanticized in folklore as a formidable lady riding a chariot with scythes on the wheels. In fact, Boudica was the wife of a chieftain of the Iceni tribe, who lived in East Anglia in Roman times. The chieftain, Prasutagus, seems to have lived in uneasy alliance with the Romans, but when he died about AD 60 he made the mistake of naming the Romans his joint heirs with his wife, Boudica, and his two daughters. No doubt he hoped by this to keep on good terms with the Romans, but in fact it had the opposite effect, for the Romans took it as a cue to rampage through Iceni lands. Dreadful insults were heaped upon the royal family, and Boudica, strong lady that she was, led a revolt. The British erupted with pent-up fury against the many injustices, and the Romans were taken aback. A large Roman town had been built to house colonizing veterans at Colchester, and Boudica's host swept down on it, overrunning the defenders and destroying all with fire and sword. A Roman legion was caught on the march and annihilated. Mad with blood-lust, the rebel host marched on London. The bulk of the Roman army was away in Wales, mopping up the last Celtic resistance there, and the city lay undefended. Roman accounts speak of thousands of civilians being put to gory deaths by the vengeful Iceni, and archaeological investigations have uncovered a pile of severed heads from the strata relating to this period.

But a reckoning was inevitable – the legions marched back from Wales, and Boudica set out to meet them. A great final battle was fought in which the Iceni, although overwhelming in numbers, were outclassed by Rome's tough professionals and mercilessly slaughtered. The Romans put down the revolt with ruthless brutality, and Boudica herself sickened and

died. She is thought to have taken poison. According to one Roman account, 'The Britons mourned her deeply, and gave her a rich burial.' The grave has never been found, and even the site of the great battle remains a matter for dispute. It seems highly likely that the Romans would have tried everything, especially torture, to find the location of Boudica's grave and despoil it. Perhaps, just perhaps, however, it escaped them. Its discovery would certainly cause an archaeological sensation, and it's difficult not to speculate on the nature of that 'rich burial'. This would presumably not include just the great gold torque she is said to have worn around her neck, nor the silver coins the Iceni minted, and which have been recovered from other caches dating from the rebellion, but also, very likely, the choicest of the loot which her followers took from the great Roman towns they sacked and ravaged.

Treasures of the Maya

Right:
Catherwood and Stephens were interested in the lost cities of the Maya, and Edward Thompson relished the gold artifacts he dredged up from the well at Chichen Itza. But today it is engraved stone inscriptions, such as this stele, which attract treasure hunters. There is a flourishing black market in stelae, stolen from remote jungle ruins at great cost to the archaeological and cultural value of the sites.

Far right:
Mayan temples at Palenque emerge as islands from the jungle growth which always threatens to engulf them. Mayan culture was in decline on the eve of the Conquest, weakened by civil war and revolt. The ruthless campaigns of the Spaniards destroyed what remained in their lust for gold, leaving only these imposing ruins as a testimony to a lost way of life.

Of all the pre-Columbian peoples of America, perhaps the Maya remain the most mysterious. From AD 400 to 1000, their civilization flourished in the Yucatán peninsula, across the countries of modern Mexico, Belize, Guatemala, Honduras, and El Salvador. It produced spectacular cities which still bear testimony to a remarkable religious, artistic, and scientific life and yet, by the time the Spanish conquistadores arrived in 1517, Mayan society had undergone such changes that it appeared to be in an advanced state of decay. Repeated military expeditions, and the introduction of European diseases to which the Maya had no natural resistance, completed the process. Thousands of Maya died and their culture collapsed. For centuries their magnificent temples were overrun by the encroaching jungle. Occasionally a passing European adventurer would seek them out, marvel at their decaying splendor, and then move on. For the most part they were largely forgotten – until, that is, they were uncovered by the pioneering work of John Lloyd Stephens and Frederick Catherwood in the mid-19th century.

First sites discovered

Stephens was an American lawyer and diplomat who had traveled widely in Asia and the Middle East, and who had developed a passion for ruins. Catherwood was a self-effacing English artist, whose sketches of Jerusalem attracted Stephens when on a visit to London. The two decided to team up to investigate tales of lost cities in the Central American jungles.

Their expeditions were brief – from 1839 to 1841 – but their adventures were varied, and the impact of their discoveries was enormous. At a time when traveling was difficult and the political situation volatile, to say the least, Stephens and Catherwood rediscovered three of the most breathtaking of the Mayan sites: Cópan, in Honduras, and Palenque and Chichen Itza in Mexico. Catherwood made remarkably accurate drawings of Mayan buildings, idols, and inscriptions, and their publication was greeted with rapturous enthusiasm. His sketches of great pyramids, overgrown with tangled bush and lianas, complex temples with trees growing from detritus on the stone steps, and statues smothered in rapacious greenery, were largely responsible for the aura of romance which continues to surround the 'lost cities of the Maya'.

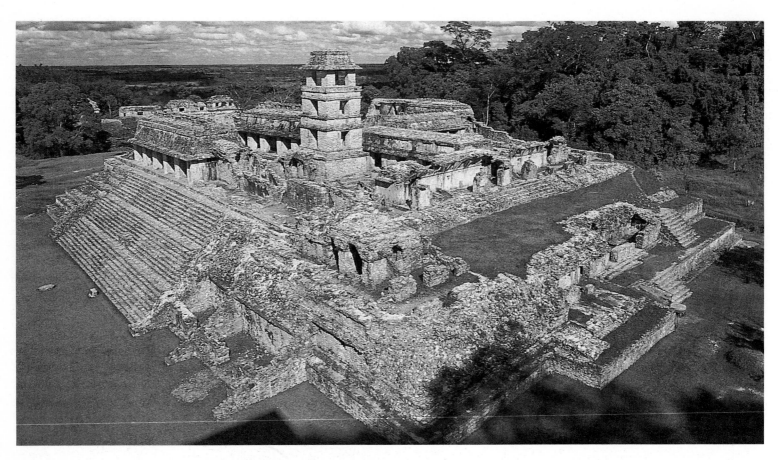

Above:
A Mayan palace at Palenque, Mexico. When Catherwood and Stephens began their expedition to the land of the Maya in 1839, the long-deserted ruins were completely overgrown by dense jungle. More recent clearance of the sites has revealed the extraordinary grandeur of Mayan architecture.

Far right:
A remarkable and rare Mayan tomb beneath the Temple of Inscriptions, Palenque. Mayan script is still largely undeciphered, but recent discoveries suggest high-ranking Mayans might have been buried with valuable grave goods. Golden artifacts of Aztec design from the north as well as indigenous Mayan work were recently found at one site.

Proofs of human sacrifice

One man who was certainly inspired by them, a generation later, was a New Englander, Edward Thompson, who first sought out the ruins to further his theory that the Maya might be the origin of the legend of Atlantis. He soon dropped that idea but was intrigued instead by a story that the Maya of Chichén Itzá used to make sacrifices, of both people and valuables, to a rain god, Yum Chac. This god inhabited a ceremonial well, or *cenote,* connected by a well-worn path to the central temple complex. The *cenote* itself was roughly oval, formed naturally by collapsing limestone strata, and was some 180 feet across. The rocky sides fell 80 feet to the great, green, unappetizing surface of the water.

The depth of the water was anybody's guess, but Thompson resolved to find out, and to test the veracity of the legend by seeking any offerings which might remain at the bottom. He obtained an antiquated mechanical scoop, and in 1904, with the aid of some local workers, he began to dredge. At first it seemed he was doomed to disappointment. Scoop after scoop revealed nothing but foul-smelling sludge, rotting vegetation and the remains of the odd animal which had fallen in and drowned. And then, as he was on the verge of giving up, Thompson scooped out a ball of copal resin, a substance known to be used by the Maya in their religious ceremonies. More copal

emerged, then a Mayan spear-throwing stick, and finally, to Thompson's delight, some human remains, indicating that the legend of human sacrifice was true. Thompson also recovered gold – small bells, with their clappers removed to 'kill' them before sacrifice, and jewelry, a golden tiara. When the scoop could retrieve no more, Thompson descended in a deep-sea diving suit, and searched the floor of the well himself. By the time he had finished, a friend estimated his finds were worth several hundreds of thousands of dollars at bullion rates alone. Thompson smuggled his treasure back to the Peabody Museum at Harvard which had sponsored him, an unwise move which outraged the Mexican authorities and led to the closure of the site. After years of legal wrangling, some of the treasure was returned to Mexico, where the authorities themselves made two efforts – in 1961/1962 and 1967 – to explore the *cenote,* raising a further 2,600 items.

And the Maya continue to intrigue. As recently as 1985 an American team working in Belize discovered a Mayan tomb dating from the time just before the Spanish conquest. Not only did it contain gold items of apparently Aztec origin, but it was of such splendor that it has forced scholars to think again of the relationships between the Central American peoples and the influence of the Maya on the immediate eve of conquest.

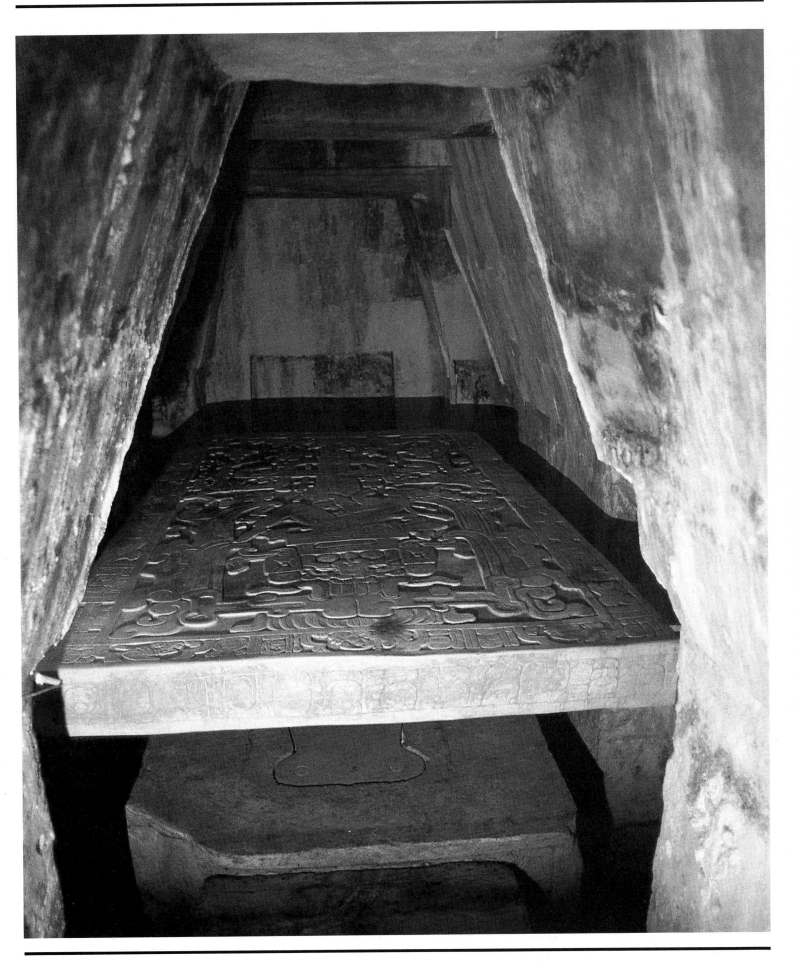

The mystery of the temple

An astonishingly convoluted story of fabulous buried treasure from ancient times comes out of a little church at Rennes le Château in the south of France. The village lies some 30 miles south of Carcassone and in earlier days was called Aereda. The Visigoths, who once ruled over southern France and part of Spain, made a last stand there in AD 501 before being routed by the Franks. The village was then abandoned and became a ruin. When it was rebuilt much later it was renamed Rennes le Château.

In the 1800s, a shepherd wandering near the village stumbled across the entrance to a cave in the hillside. He was chasing a straying lamb into the cave and all at once found himself surrounded by dozens of skeletons and chests crammed with gold coins. The shepherd was understandably terrified but not too scared to fill his pockets with all the coins he could carry before running home. Rather unwisely, he told the villagers the source of his newfound wealth but refused to reveal the location of the hoard. The villagers ridiculed such a patent fiction and had him executed for theft.

Nothing more was heard of the treasure for some years. Then, in 1885, a new parish priest arrived in the village. His name was Beranger Saunière. He soon became a very close friend of a neighbor's teenage daughter, Marie Denarnaud, and from that time she became his inseparable companion, helping him to run the church.

Priceless parchments

In 1891 Beranger put some restoration work in hand on the altar and the roof of the church, with the aid of a grant. Babon, the stonemason working on the job, found that one of the altar pillars was hollow, and inside it were hidden some wooden, wax-sealed rolls. When Beranger opened one of these he found in it a parchment written in Latin and French.

Beranger spent some time studying all the parchments. When the mayor turned up demanding to know what it was all about Beranger, realizing that the man would not be able to understand the parchments, showed them to him, explaining that they were useless documents concerning the Revolution. Suddenly, Beranger put a stop to all restoration work. He left some of the parchments in Paris with experts on ancient manuscripts. From the ones he kept to himself he gleaned enough to send him hastily to the Louvre, where he bought a copy of a painting by Nicolas Poussin

Far left:
The little village of Rennes le Château, in southern France, was the scene of bitter fighting in centuries past. Today its fame rests largely on the astonishing wealth suddenly and secretly acquired by its originally unassuming parish priest around the turn of the century. Nobody has for certain solved the mystery of this ecclesiastical windfall, but rumor has it that the cleric stumbled on some of the treasure from Jerusalem, hidden perhaps long ago by the Knights Templar.

called *Shepherds of Arcadia*. When he got back to his village he was convinced that a treasure lay beneath the church. He told Marie about it, and together they tried to find it.

The instructions in the documents were anything but straightforward. There were measurements in fathoms, leading from the altar, and references to a particular tomb in the churchyard. Beranger and Marie eventually managed to decipher the peculiar inscriptions on the gravestone, and in conjunction with further instructions, began to dig. They seem to have calculated correctly because they soon found the lost treasure vault.

Beranger prospers

Suddenly, from being virtually a pauper, Beranger seemed to have untold wealth at his fingertips. The church restoration was resumed on a far grander scale, with the priest paying for it all out of his own pocket. All kinds of welcome and expensive amenities were added to the village, and Marie lived in high style, entertaining the cream of society. It is thought that Beranger shrewdly disposed of quantities of the treasure in various parts of Europe. But he was also careful to keep the location secret by assiduously defacing the clues on the gravestone.

As Beranger continued to buy property and land, he put it all in Marie's name. Both the mayor and the Bishop of Carcassone called on Beranger to demand an explanation for this sudden wealth. The priest wined and dined them extravagantly, explaining that he had inherited his riches from a recently deceased relative. When he reinforced this story with a persuasive parting bribe, both worthy gentlemen seemed to be satisfied.

In 1897, Beranger built himself an enormous villa, in which he installed himself in great luxury at a reputed cost of a million francs. But by now a new bishop had taken over. He was made of sterner stuff and, disbelieving the old priest's tale, eventually had him suspended from office. When a new parish priest arrived in the village Beranger simply ignored him and the bishop, and carried on as usual, supported by his ecstatic villagers.

In January 1917 he paid out 8 million francs for a water supply to be laid on for Rennes le Château. It was his last act of beneficence because a few days later he was dead – of cirrhosis of the liver. Marie became the sole beneficiary of the mysterious treasure.

Marie probably never revisited the hidden vault; she had more than enough money to last for the rest of her life. For about a quarter of a century thereafter she shut herself away. But in 1946 she confided the whole story to a Monsieur Corbu and his wife, who came to live with her. She eventually bequeathed her house

Far right:
A shaft of sunlight illumines the inside of the dome of the Church of the Holy Sepulcher in Jerusalem. It was one of the holy places in Palestine that the Crusaders, together with 20,000 fighting Knights Templar, liberated and restored to Christianity. The Knights Templar were the richest and most powerful of all the medieval Christians, and at one time owned more than 8,000 castles. Many of these were spread throughout France and it is rumored that vast fortunes still lie hidden in some of them.

'Shepherds in Arcadia', painted by the French artist Nicolas Poussin, seemingly embodied a vital clue to a vast treasure hoard hidden at Rennes le Château. Poussin depicts some shepherds kneeling at a tomb.

to them and said she would tell them where the treasure lay just before she died. Regrettably, on 18th January 1953, Marie, by that time in her eighties, fell into a coma and died without recovering consciousness.

Clues point to Poussin's painting

There is no shortage of clues as to the location of the vault. Among the deciphered parchments one reads: 'This treasure belongs to Dagobert II, King, and to Sion, and he is here dead.' The code in the second parchment proved to be astonishingly complex, but the message eventually read: 'Shepherdess no temptation to which Poussin Teniers hold the key peace 681 by the cross of this horse of God I complete this daemon guardian at midday blue apples.' It is a perfect anagram of the inscription on the headstone which Beranger had been at such pains to scrub out. Unknown to him, the text had previously been copied and published before he began to cover his trail.

Poussin's painting corresponds almost exactly with the view from Rennes le Château. There were other clues which indicated that Poussin

VOUS TOUS QUI SOUFFREZ QUI ETES ACCABLES ET JE VO
EZ A MOI

was linked in some way with the secret. An American author, Henry Lincoln, who has made this mystery a life study, has unearthed much more significant material. He discovered, for example, that King Dagobert II was one of the last monarchs of the Merovingian dynasty. He was able to trace a direct link from the Franks (over whom Dagobert reigned) back to the destruction by the Romans of Jerusalem in AD 70. At that time the fabulous treasure of King Solomon's Temple was carried off by the victors. Could the hoard first discovered by the unfortunate shepherd and later by Beranger be the whole or part of the Jerusalem treasure?

In spite of tempting clues pointing strongly in that direction, Lincoln thinks not. He believes there is much stronger evidence linking the treasure with the mystical Order of Rosicrucians and the secrets of alchemy. He is convinced that Beranger underwent a dramatic change of belief, secretly abandoning his faith for something akin to devil worship. Lincoln suggests that Beranger's riches did not come from buried treasure but from resources amply supplied to him by the Priory of Sion, that is, the Rosicrucians.

Opposing this theory is the testimony of Marie, who steadfastly averred that the vault existed and was still well supplied with treasure.

Above:
This painting faces the altar in the church at Rennes le Château. The church and churchyard abound with clues to the site of a massive treasure hoard: possibly one is contained in the painting, but the mystery has not been solved.

The legacy of the Jesuits

Treasure scented with a whiff of ecclesiasticism has been most prominently linked with that militant religious order, the Society of Jesus, popularly known as the Jesuits. The order was founded in 1534 by St Ignatius Loyola, and approved six years later by Pope Paul III. Pledged to a life of poverty, chastity, and obedience, the Jesuits rapidly grew in power and prestige both politically and economically.

King Philip II of Spain, uneasy at what he saw as a threat, curbed their control of wealth in Spain by means of a law passed in 1592. But Jesuit missionaries merely fanned out farther afield, concentrating particularly on the New World. This meant a vast region of Spanish colonies stretching from Colorado in the north to Bolivia in the south. In many of these areas mineral wealth abounded. The Jesuits established missions and mines in all these places, seeking both to save the souls of the uncivilized Indians who lived there and

recruiting a convenient labor force to extract gold and silver from under the ground.

When the Spanish Crown got to hear of this bonanza, it not unnaturally wanted its cut, and promptly slapped a 20 percent tax (known as the Royal Fifth) on all New World takings. The reaction of the missionaries was predictably less than halfhearted and soon they were practicing many ingenious fiddles to outwit the treasury. Things got so bad that a break was inevitable. Many prudent Jesuits began to hoard piles of silver and gold instead of sending it back to Europe, and were content to await the outcome. Finally, the Spanish Crown lost all patience and in 1767 expelled the order from Latin America. Before the missionaries left the New World (hoping doubtless to return before long) they carefully camouflaged the various caves, vaults, and other hiding places which concealed their continuously amassed treasure. The expulsion order of 1767 also applied in

Spain, Portugal, and France, and six years later the Society of Jesus was completely suppressed, reviving in 1814.

From that time onwards, rumors and legends of huge hoards of Jesuit treasure lying in many parts of North and South America have spread like prairie fires. Various expeditions have gone forth looking for this wealth, but so far as is known, not one of them has succeeded.

Particularly persistent rumors have circulated about a magnificent silver mine, discovered in 1736, and adjudged to be located somewhere in Arizona. The mine was called La Purísima Concepción, and was said to lie slightly south of the Cerro Ruido Mountains. In 1750, the local Indians revolted, burned down the mission, and threw out the Spanish authorities. But four years later the mine was reopened.

A rancher recently unearthed some ancient documents relating to the mine. They are specific in detailed description but unfortunately

hazy in precise instructions as to its whereabouts. Among other things, they pinpoint La Purísima Concepción in relation to a Guadelupe mine, but there are many mines bearing that title all over the Southwest. The measurements, too, are unclear. But there are strong hints that the mine lies not far from the Tumacacori mission, a protected national monument on the east bank of the Rio Santa Cruz, about 48 miles south of Tucson.

Indian legends tell of a rich mine somewhere in the 6,000-foot Cerro Ruido Peak. Not long after the end of World War I, two unnamed army veterans decided to do some prospecting there. They parted company for a few days while one man set off to explore Tucson and the other stayed on the mountain. When they next met, the man who had stayed behind told his friend that he had found what appeared to be man-made excavations of some kind. The two of them examined the piles of rocks and dirt at

Above:
A spectacular storm over Tucson, Arizona, lights up the sky. Such storms not uncommonly cause flash floods in the hills and completely change the face of the landscape in a matter of hours. Treasure-hunters, having pinpointed the location of a possible hoard in a derelict mine, have returned after a violent storm to find all their familiar landmarks completely washed away and the hills once more hiding their secret caches of silver and gold.

Above:
These 17th-century church carvings were executed by unlettered Guaraní Indians in Paraguay, under the supervision of Jesuit instructors.

the bottom of a ledge but, because they were running short of supplies, one of them volunteered to go into Nogales to restock. When he got back he found his friend asleep under a tree, his body scratched and clothing torn.

His friend told him a fantastic story. After toiling for some hours on the debris below the ledge, he had finally uncovered the entrance to a cave carved out of the rock. The following day he entered the cave and found himself in a long, dark, dusty tunnel which he reckoned to extend to about 400 feet (120m). By the light of his carbide lamp he could make out the outline of a heap of sacks against the wall. He opened one sack and found it held crude silver ore. At a rough count, he guessed there might be as much as 30 tons of the stuff lying there. He also noted that there were several smaller branches leading off the main shaft.

Deciding to leave things as they were until his friend returned, the man spent the next day exploring another canyon. There he suddenly came across a small opening covered with dried vegetation. Beyond it, in a clearing, stood the ruins of an ancient small church. It was crumbling and overgrown, but the man realized that it must be the remains of an old mission, probably linked to the mine he had stumbled on the previous day.

He photographed the scene, then made camp for the night. He was quite unable to get to sleep, however, because of some nameless dread that seemed to envelop him. This grew stronger by the minute until it reached the proportions of terror. Suddenly a ghastly scream re-echoed down the canyon. The man waited no longer. In sheer panic he leapt to his feet and raced back to his main campsite by the mine, crashing into boulders and tearing his clothes on thorns and bushes. Completely worn out, he collapsed under a tree and lay there until woken by his companion.

His friend dismissed the whole story as a nightmare, but the man insisted that he had not been dreaming and promised he could prove it when the film in his camera was developed. But the exciting silver mine obviously took priority. They removed a sample of the ore, and the nightmare man again elected to stay behind while his friend traveled once more into Tucson to have the sample assayed. He also took the camera with him to have the film developed.

As this man left the mountain, he became aware of a tremendous storm brewing up behind him. He turned, and using up the last remaining frame on the film roll, snapped a picture of the storm clouds over the Cerro Ruido. The assay was completed. Deeply disturbed by reports of floods and other storm havoc in the mountains, the man rushed back to look for his friend. On the way he collected the

MACULA NON EST IN TE

prints from the camera but didn't bother to look at them. He found the landscape quite drastically changed, with landslides, rock falls, and obliterated trails all adding to the confusion. He searched in vain for his companion, and in spite of weeks of effort with the help of teams from Nogales, no trace of him was ever found.

When eventually the survivor came to examine the photographs, he found pictures of the ruins of the old mission just as described, and another of the cave entrance to the lost mine. There was also his own picture of the storm clouds over the Cerro Ruido.

Years later, in 1958, he appeared on television to confirm the story, but still insisted on remaining anonymous. The lost mine and mission are still there, presumably, for the finding.

Above:
Part of the restored altar in an 18th-century church at Concepción, Bolivia. The church was founded by the Jesuits during their missionary drive in the New World.

Chapter 5

The Spoils of War

For the past 3,000 years or so, the taking
of spoils in the form of precious objects
has been the privilege of conquerors,
both to aggrandize themselves and to
reward their followers. By the same token, the
conquered have tried to conceal their valuables
in the hope that those will sustain them in
uncertain days ahead. This millennia-old game
of hide-and-seek provides us with some of the
most fascinating lost treasures of the world, and
some of the most spectacular treasures to have
been found. The hunt takes us from the warrior-
horsemen of ancient Thrace, on the shores of
the Black Sea, to the Germany of Adolf Hitler.

The Thracian civilization was established in
and around present-day Bulgaria by about 3500
BC, and there is evidence that it was working
locally mined gold at that time – after Egypt,
perhaps the oldest-known culture to do so.
Certainly, by about 500 BC, the Thracians were
producing magnificent gold and silver artifacts
that had no contemporary equivalent
anywhere. Most of those so far found come
from tombs and graveyards, but in 1985/1986,
a new hoard came to light in the village of
Rogozen, in northwest Bulgaria, in unusual
circumstances. For the 165 silver-gilt items were
not associated with a grave. Initial investigation
suggested that they had been buried sometime
after the middle of the 4th century BC at a time
when Philip II of Macedon was conquering
Thrace. The inference is that they were hidden
from the invaders by a chieftain later killed or
captured in battle with the Greeks – one of the
earliest known concealments of riches for such
reasons.

Golden ark
Another may have taken place more than 150
years previously, in what is now Israel and
Jordan, and if that treasure were to be found it
could be the most spectacular discovery of all
time – worth a staggering $900 million or more,
according to some experts. In 586 BC, King
Nebuchadnezzar of Babylon stormed
Jerusalem, sacking the city and its Temple of
Solomon and carrying the Jews off into
captivity; there is evidence that before the
Babylonians arrived, the Jews managed to
conceal a great deal of their secular and
religious wealth, perhaps even including the
long-sought golden Ark of the Covenant, in
which the most sacred Jewish writings
were kept.

The evidence is adduced by authors such as
René Noorbergen from materials recovered
from Qumran, where the religious writings
known as the Dead Sea Scrolls were
accidentally discovered in 1947. The materials
on which Noorbergen draws are not part of the
scrolls, but were found some five years later,
and are engraved on thin copper sheets, rather
than parchment. Translated, they list, according
to Noorbergen and his fellow-writer John Marc
Allegro, 61 sites in the Holy Land where
treasure is buried, including a total of nearly
97,000 pounds of gold and 338,000 pounds of
silver. There is nothing to connect this list with
Nebuchadnezzar's invasion other than surmise,
but the case for doing so appears plausible.
Unfortunately, the descriptions of the sites are
very vague: 'There is a money chest in the
fortress in the Vale of Anchor containing 17

talents (a talent is about 75 pounds US), hidden 40 cubits under the steps of the eastern entrance', according to one account (the full list is in Noorbergen's *Treasures of the Lost Races*). As yet, nobody has succeeded in relating the descriptions sufficiently closely to the modern landscape to find any of the caches.

Luck, sometimes assisted by intelligent guesswork, has played a large part in the discovery, for example in Britain, France, and elsewhere, of hoards buried by wealthy Romans as their western empire crumbled under the barbarian onslaughts between about AD 161 and AD 476. There were no written records to lead investigators to caches such as England's Mildenhall Treasure or the many Roman items of the 4th century found piecemeal since 1731 at Corbridge on the River Tyne. Plenty more hoards of this period must exist in Europe, although there are few clues to where precisely they are.

According to various legends the barbarian hordes that raided or conquered the centers of civilization left behind lots of treasure. Alaric, leader of the Visigoths who sacked Rome in 410, is said to have pillaged virtually all of the city's treasure. Attila the Hun, who died in 453 and was another scourge of the collapsing western empire, acquired great wealth during his campaign in the Balkans, according to legend. The 12th-century epic poem *Nibelunglied,* in which Attila appears as Etzel, speaks both of the treasures he owned and of his insatiable greed for more. No one knows what these treasures may have been, nor where they are now. Similar tales attached themselves

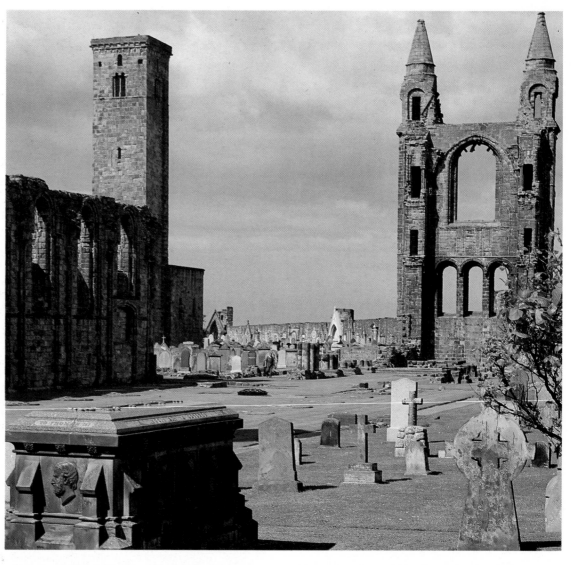

Right:
Robert the Bruce, King of Scotland and leader of the Scottish army that vanquished the English at Bannockburn in 1314, shortly afterwards attended the consecration of the cathedral at St Andrews, where he gave thanks for his victory. According to legend, Robert left more tangible tokens of appreciation, too – a hoard of valuables taken from the defeated enemy. It is said to lie in a vault under the ruins.

Top far right:
The majestic ruins of Corfe Castle dominate the countryside near Wareham, Dorset, southern England. During the Civil War, the owner, Lady Mary Bankes, is said to have concealed the family fortune in a well, which she then blew up to prevent Cromwell's troops from finding it.

Far right:
This beautiful 16th-century miniature – a treasure in its own right – shows the Mongol hordes of Genghis Khan besieging an unnamed Chinese town during Genghis's all-conquering career. The miniature comes from a history compiled in Persia and completed in 1596.

to Genghis Khan and his grandson Kublai Khan, whose Mongol followers overran much of central Asia and threatened the portals of eastern Europe in the 13th century, and to Tamerlane, who emulated their feats in southern Asia from 1369. However, here we are on somewhat surer ground. The Venetian traveller Marco Polo described at first hand the wonders of Kublai Khan's summer capital of Shang-tu (the Xanadu of poetry and myth), including an entire hillside decorated with semi-precious lapis lazuli to delight the Khan's eye. Since the mid-19th century, explorers and archaeologists have been investigating the Mongol territories, making some spectacular finds. But they have not yet traced the treasure hoard of Genghis Khan, said to lie somewhere in the arid steppes of central Asia, nor the gold and other valuables of Tamerlane, hidden outside his capital city of Samarkand.

The records of the monks
The spread of Christianity throughout western Europe contributed, as a by-product, to our

knowledge of the treasures pillaged by marauders in the first millennium AD, for two reasons. The monasteries of the Dark and Middle Ages were the repositories of learning, the only places where written records of everyday events were kept, and many of those records have survived. And, as the monasteries and their associated churches grew richer, they became a natural focus for armies or bands of raiders in search of booty.

Ecclesiastical accounts, for example, tell us a great deal about the depredations of the Vikings, whose longships terrorized the coasts of Britain, Ireland, and France from the 8th century onward, and eventually carried them through the Mediterranean toward Constantinople. At Lindisfarne, off England's northeast coast, a surprise raid in AD 793 left the church 'despoiled of all its ornaments' – jeweled caskets, valuable statuary, rich vestments, and much more – says a contemporary report.

At Rouen in France in 841, the Vikings plundered the monasteries, slew the monks, and extorted gold and silver from the ordinary inhabitants as the price for their departure.

From the middle of the 9th century the Vikings raided Spain, Portugal, southern France, Italy, and the Arab lands of North Africa, looting and exacting tribute. Their first attacks came as a complete surprise, giving the victims little time to hide their most precious objects. Later, however, it seems some valuables were concealed, among them perhaps a gold-and-silver 8th-century chalice found at Ardagh in Ireland in 1868.

Legends of treasure hidden from the Vikings abound in western Europe, but a bigger mystery surrounds the spoils they took, which must have amounted to a massive fortune over the years. The Frankish kings are recorded to have paid over 685 pounds of gold and 43,000 pounds of silver in tribute alone. The English contributed tens of millions of predominantly silver coins in Danegelt (a form of tax, levied as 'protection' against Viking raids), and lesser quantities of silver came from North Africa and from Germany. Yet very little of this treasure has been found.

A thousand or so relatively small hoards have been traced in Scandinavia, including some 60,000 coins of Arab silver and others of Frankish and English origin. The biggest Viking silver cache of all – weighing 88 pounds and four times larger than any other – was unearthed at Cuerdale in northwest England in 1840, and was seemingly the war-chest of a 10th-century leader. The largest gold cache of Viking origin, weighing just 10 pounds, was found on an island in the River Shannon in Ireland in the 19th century. Some of the Vikings' booty must have been lost in shipwrecks such as the one off the Shetland Isles in 1151. Nevertheless, much still remains to be accounted for.

Conquests and discoveries

Between 1095, when Pope Urban II preached the First Crusade to free Jerusalem from the Turks, and 1580, when Francis Drake completed his voyage around the world, the previously inward-looking western Europeans spread their developing techniques of warfare across the globe, although this expansion did not prevent them from doing battle with each other at home. At the same time, as we have seen, stirrings in Asia threw up a succession of Mongol rulers whose names became synonymous with pillage.

The early part of this period brought the flowering of the feudal system, with powerful barons conducting their affairs from great castles and bearing only nominal fealty to overlords and kings, while constantly vying with each other for riches and power. Their activities have given rise to many tales of hidden spoils – in Scotland, for example, hoards of valuable 14th-century coins hidden by warring leaders have come to light at Montrave and elsewhere, and another massive treasure is said to lie underground at Roslin Castle. The ruins of St Andrew's Cathedral reputedly guard an immense collection of booty captured from the defeated English at the Battle of Bannockburn in 1314.

The loot from Europe's feudal struggles, however, all fades in comparison with the wholesale slaughter and pillaging that accompanied European colonization of the Americas, in particular by the Spaniards. Earlier chapters have recounted the history of the treasure-fleets and the brutalities associated with the first searches for El Dorado. However, there are many who believe that the conquistadores succeeded in wresting away only a fraction of the gold and silver of the civilizations they encountered, while much more was hidden to keep it from the invaders.

For example, in 1971 investigators found a massive system of tunnels, more than 50 miles long, leading from Mount Huascarán in the Peruvian Andes westwards to the Pacific Coast. Tradition says the tunnels were used as an underground treasure-store by the beleaguered Incas, though as yet no treasure has been revealed. One theory is that they originally carried on beneath the ocean to the offshore island of Guanape, and that somewhere in this last stretch, now flooded, is a huge vault stacked with the Incas' wealth.

Another legend asserts that the Aztecs of Central America also tried to thwart the Spaniards by hiding their most prized possessions in remote jungle temples. Among them are, reputedly, 52 golden tablets comprising a history of Central America, somewhere in the region of Tenochtitlán.

Civil wars and revolutions

The 17th and 18th centuries brought massive upheavals in the established order in Europe and some of its colonies, beginning with the Thirty Years' War of 1618-48 and the English Civil War of 1642-51, and culminating in the American and French revolutions of 1776 and 1789 respectively. During this epoch, however, attitudes towards pillage, in the west at least, began to change, though races regarded as 'inferior', such as those of South America and later Africa, remained fair game. So did vulnerable and valuable cargoes on the high seas. But Europe itself was not subject to depredations on the scale practiced by the likes of Alaric or the Vikings. Various factors contributed to this gradual evolution: the publication, by the Dutchman Hugo Grotius in 1625, of a treatise regarded as the foundation of the rules of war and of the settlement of international disputes; a more enlightened

US Private Ernest Garrison guards part of the looted art collection amassed by Hermann Goering, who acquired vast numbers of priceless paintings from all over Europe, and displayed some of them at his home, Karinhall, in Berlin. Just before Germany's final defeat, the treasures were rushed by train to a secret cave near Königsee in the Bavarian Alps for safekeeping. But shortly afterwards Goering revealed their hiding-place to the US Military Government.

Below:
The Mongol chieftain Genghis Khan (?1167-1227) built an empire covering most of southern Asia from the Black Sea in the west to the Yellow Sea in the east. According to legend, he concealed a treasure hoard somewhere in the vast, dry Asian steppes.

Top far left:
The castle of Veldenstein in Germany was another hiding-place for Goering's booty. A Polish former concentration camp inmate helped the Allies to locate some of the treasures concealed there in 1945, including 36 priceless candlesticks. But, he said, there was more to be found.

Far left:
Hermann Goering (1893-1946), photographed in 1940, the year in which he was appointed Reichsmarschall. He directed the Luftwaffe (air force) in the Blitz, a bombing campaign that brought Britain close to defeat in the summer and fall of 1940.

attitude, a product of the Age of Reason, towards the treasures of other nations; and the spreading use of paper money, whose value could be canceled at the stroke of a pen.

None of this was immediately clear, of course, to those caught up in the English Civil War. The west of England and Wales, in particular, are reputed to house still unrecovered treasures hidden from the parliamentary forces of Oliver Cromwell. At Corfe Castle in Dorset, a fortune is believed to lie at the bottom of a well, hurled there for safety by the owner, who then dynamited it over. On the parliamentary side, John Barkstead, put in charge of the Tower of London by Oliver Cromwell, used the opportunity to extract all the valuables he could from the Royalist prisoners held there. Barkstead's spoils are thought to have been hidden in the Tower, but have not been found.

The two great revolutions in the last quarter of the 18th century began among what we would call today the middle classes, who were more concerned with political and civil rights than with the seizure of booty for its own sake. The American Revolution continued in that vein, and produced few tales of hidden treasures. The French Revolution and its immediate aftermath drew in the urban poor and at least some of the peasantry, but events such as the incursions into the palaces of

Versailles and the Tuileries were marked more by wanton destruction and small-scale theft than by mass pillaging. The same was eventually true of the Russian Revolution of 1917, although not of the civil war that followed.

Fleeing French aristocrats took what they could carry with them in the way of valuables – Marie Antoinette, captured before she could get out of France, had jewelry and a silver dinner service – and may have concealed more at home. Some French stately homes have unproven legends to that effect. But in general, relatively little disappeared without trace. This apparent restraint continued into the Napoleonic era. For still-missing treasures lost in war, we now have to look to our own century – in particular to the depredations of the Nazis – or outside Europe.

African hoard
The discovery of diamonds at Kimberley in 1869 and gold on the Witwatersrand in 1886 brought prospectors, speculators, and adventurers flocking from all over the world to what is now South Africa, in search of their fortunes. Among them was the Englishman Cecil Rhodes. Rhodes' ambition was boundless, and in the mid-1880s his British South Africa Company obtained mining rights in Matabeleland (Ndebeland) from the local king, Lobengula.

Above:
Oliver Cromwell (1599-1658) and his Parliamentarian army survey the field of victory at Marston Moor, during the English Civil War. The battle, in 1644, was the first defeat for Charles I's Royalist cavalry. England abounds in stories of treasures hidden during this troubled period of her history, when countless items of gold and silver were melted down to help finance the Royalist cause.

Despite their agreement, relations between Rhodes and Lobengula soon grew sour, as it became clear that the Englishman intended to annex Matabeleland and its neighboring regions for the British crown. Before that, however, open warfare had broken out between the troops of Rhodes' company and Lobengula's Matabele.

There is some evidence to show that the Matabele king had prepared for the conflict by instructing those of his subjects who flocked south for work in the mines to smuggle back what they could in the form of diamonds and gold. At any rate, Lobengula had amassed a fortune in bullion, coins, gold dust, diamonds, and ivory valued at $14 million at the time.

Inevitably, the Matabele were defeated, but when company troops entered the tribal capital of Bulawayo in 1893, there was no sign of Lobengula and only a small portion of the gold.

Lobengula had apparently fled with the treasure up the valley of the Zambesi River, and simply disappeared, never to be seen again. Rumor said that he had hidden his wealth at the source of the Kori River, but an expedition in the 1920s failed to find the cache – perhaps because there are two waterways of the same name in the region and it chose the wrong one. Some versions of the tale maintain that Lobengula, nearing death and with few loyal followers left, chose to be walled up in a mountain cave with the treasure.

Top:
The Cuerdale hoard of Viking silver was found by 19th-century laborers shoring up the banks of the River Ribble in north-west England, and contained more than 7,000 coins, as well as fibulae (brooches), chains and other items of jewelry.

Left:
This magnificent example of an Iron Age torque, or neck ring, adorned a Celtic warrior in Britain during the 1st century BC. It is made from electrum, an alloy of gold and silver, and was found at Ken Hill, near Snettisham in Norfolk, England. The torque is now on display at the British Museum in London.

Bottom:
Six more examples of Celtic torques found at Ipswich, Suffolk, in eastern England. Although the designs are all broadly similar, each example is slightly different, perhaps reflecting the individual preferences of the original owners, members of the warrior class.

An imperial fortune

Right:

Right:
Ill-starred Tsar Nicholas II (1868-1918) appears resplendent in medieval imperial dress. He, too, is said to have died at Ekaterinburg. However, the only item linked to him, and that tentatively, in the alleged mineshaft grave was a belt-buckle. The absence of firm evidence of his death has led to continued speculation that he survived in anonymity, perhaps for years.

Right:
The last Tsarina of Russia, German-born Alexandra Feodorovna (1872-1918), contributed to the downfall of the Russian monarchy by the weight she attributed to the opinions of the peasant mystic Grigory Rasputin. Like the rest of the imperial family, Alexandra is said to have been murdered by the Bolsheviks in July 1918 at Ekaterinburg, and her remains cast into a mineshaft. Items belonging to her recovered from the mine include a cross of emeralds, diamonds and pearls set in platinum. But her body has never been found.

The tangled events of the Russian Revolution of 1917 and the ensuing civil war between the Bolsheviks and their opponents' the White Army, have produced more tales of lost treasure than any other single chapter of 20th-century history. The thousands of aristocrats and prosperous merchants fleeing abroad took what personal wealth they could carry with them, often claiming to have left fortunes in valuable items concealed at home against the possibility of returning later. In Russia, the armies of both sides as well as the fearsome bandit chiefs of Siberia, who owed allegiance to neither side, plundered the deserted estates, banks, stores, and other buildings for what they could get. In the case of the two armies, the riches were needed to sustain their war efforts; for the bandits, the motive was purely greed.

Many of these tales should be treated with extreme caution. Among the emigrés, pitchforked out of their previously comfortable existences, there were many who invented yarns of abandoned wealth, hoping to con the gullible and greedy into supporting them. However, there is considerable evidence to show that the most fabulous treasure of all did exist, and at least a reasonable possibility that a portion of it remains hidden somewhere, its secret still to be revealed.

The hoard is known by a variety of names – the Romanov gold, Kolchak's gold, the treasure of the White Army – and is commonly discussed as if it were one massive collection of platinum, gold, silver, jewels, and other items. In fact, it was three separate collections, and their fates, so far as is known, were completely different, although the second and third may to some extent have coalesced.

The fate of the Romanovs

The first represents the personal fortunes of the last Tsar, Nicholas II, and other members of the imperial Romanov family, together with jewelry belonging to the crown. The crown jewels were rapidly seized by the Bolsheviks; some were sold, and the rest are now on display in the Kremlin. The Romanovs' own fortune in Russia in 1917 amounted perhaps to $4 million. Some of it was used to pay the expenses of Nicholas, his wife, and children during their house-arrest at Tobolsk and Ekaterinburg (now Sverdlovsk), and much of the rest was confiscated by the Bolsheviks. Items of the Royal Family's personal jewelry were found at Ekaterinburg, after the Tsar and his immediate relations were massacred there in 1918, according to official versions of events. Many people have challenged the account of the Ekaterinburg killings. Alternative versions spare the entire family, who then lived abroad incognito; or spare all save Nicholas himself, who may have been killed at Ekaterinburg or somewhere else; or allow Anastasia, the youngest crown princess, to escape. There are other theories, too, but none has been satisfactorily proved.

That would seem to account for most of the Romanov effects in Russia itself. However, it is known that members of the family made deposits abroad in the years before World War I, and there are persistent reports of a fortune in gold lying in a bank somewhere outside Russia, awaiting a legitimate claimant. It was perhaps part of an attempt to obtain these that led Anna Anderson, a German, and a number of other women to assert that each was the miraculously spared Anastasia, right up to the 1970s. All were regarded as impostors by surviving relatives of the Romanovs.

Some money does lie in a bank in East Berlin, but the collapse of the German mark between the wars made it virtually valueless. A more favored site for the gold is the Bank of England in London; however, bank officials have consistently denied that it is there. A possible explanation, for which there is historical evidence, is that deposits were made before 1914, but withdrawn in 1915 to help the Russian war effort.

The remains of the treasure
The second, and by far larger, portion of the treasure was mainly state funds, moved around by the White Army as it struggled against the Bolsheviks and supplemented by other valuables acquired in the towns where it rested temporarily – among them Ekaterinburg, Perm, some 200 miles to the northwest, and Kazan, some 300 miles southwest of Perm. In the shifting tides of the Civil War, it is impossible to keep close track of the treasure's movements.

However, there are reports of large quantities of gold and other valuables being captured by the Bolsheviks when they took Ekaterinburg, and then being transported by rail to Perm on 17th July 1918 – the day after the supposed massacre of the Romanovs, and just before Ekaterinburg fell again to the Whites. This collection seems to have been a mixture of the Romanovs' personal wealth, state property, and appropriated gold. Part was found when the

Whites recaptured Perm, but the rest disappeared, presumably moved by the Bolsheviks.

At virtually the same time, Kazan capitulated to the Whites. Here, too, was a vast treasure-store, deposited before the Revolution to keep it from the invading Germans. The Bolsheviks had either not discovered it or been unable to move it. According to one account, it was worth more than $1 billion at contemporary values, and consisted of gold bullion, platinum, jewels, stocks, and bonds. This vast fortune, perhaps supplemented eventually by the prize from Perm, was moved eastwards by rail, deep into the fastnesses of Siberia, where Admiral Alexander Kolchak, leader of the Whites and titular Supreme Ruler of All the Russias, had his headquarters. With that transfer, the next stage in the quest for the imperial fortune begins.

Above:
The Grand Duchesses Olga and Tatiana, daughters of Nicholas and Alexandra, at work with other members of the imperial family in the grounds of the royal palace at Tsarskoe Selo, south of St Petersburg (now Leningrad), in the first phase of their captivity. They dug up part of a lawn to make a vegetable garden. In August 1917, the royal prisoners were transferred to Tobolsk in Siberia, and in April 1918 they were moved again, to Ekaterinburg.

King John's missing regalia

John, King of England from 1199 to 1216, is probably one of the most reviled monarchs in history, even though it was in his reign that the Magna Carta, a cornerstone of British freedom, was drawn up. His continuing power-struggle with the barons, alleged responsibility for the murder of his nephew Arthur of Brittany, quarrels with the Pope, and unsuccessful military campaign in France all stain his rule. On top of that, he became the only English monarch to have lost the country's crown jewels in their entirety, setting off a treasure-hunt that has gone on, without result, for more than 700 years.

The details of how that happened are obscure, but the salient facts are known. In October 1216, John was once again in the middle of a dispute with his nobles, and a rebellion against his authority had broken out in the Midland counties. The King marched north from London to quell the uprising, accompanied by his loyal troops and a baggage train containing, among other things, his royal regalia, that of his grandmother, the Empress of Germany, and a fortune in gold and jewels. In the early part of the month the entourage halted at King's Lynn, an ancient port in what was then the richest area of England.

In those days, King's Lynn lay practically on the shores of the Wash, a broad, shallow North Sea inlet between Lincolnshire and Norfolk on the east coast. Its edges then were shifting, unpredictable banks of sand, liable to frequent flooding. On 12th October, the cumbersome baggage train set out across these, southwest to Wisbech for a rendezvous with John, who, it is thought, had gone there by a longer, but safer, route.

Swallowed by the sea

Somewhere on the sandbanks disaster struck. A fast-running tide engulfed men, horses, and the treasure. By some accounts, everything was lost; others say that many of the valuables were saved and hurriedly loaded onto rescue ships. Whatever the truth, none of the regalia, gold, or jewels was ever seen again. John himself died of a fever at Newark a few days afterwards, practically penniless from the loss.

Since then, historians, archaeologists and treasure-seekers have tried to work out the exact route the baggage-train took on that fatal day, and therefore where the treasure itself may be. They are hampered in their task because much of the southwest fringe of the Wash has

Left:
This highly romanticized turn-of-the-century painting, now in the House of Commons in London, shows King John presented with the Magna Carta by the English barons at Runnymede on the River Thames in 1215. Contrary to popular belief, John did not sign the document, but signaled his acceptance of its terms by affixing his seal. It brought him little respite, and by 1216 he was at war with the feudal lords again in a campaign that cost him first his treasure and, shortly afterwards, his life.

Far left:
King John's Cup, displayed in King's Lynn, Norfolk, in eastern England, is often supposed to be part of the treasure the unfortunate monarch lost in the waters of the Wash. But expert examination shows that it dates from at least 70 years after his death.

been drained since the 13th century, including the possible paths the baggage-train may have followed, and there is considerable disagreement over the likely site of the accident.

Seeking the lost trail

It seems reasonable to assume that the party headed first for one of the villages on the west bank of a tongue of dry land between the Great Ouse River and the Wellstream, a strip of water into which several rivers drain. That would have brought the baggage-train to the villages of Cross Keys, Walpole or, the most southerly point, Walsoken. To reach the first two they would have had to cross the sandbanks at the mouth of the Great Ouse. If Walsoken was the immediate destination, they could have crossed the Great Ouse estuary at a narrow point higher up, and made most of the journey on land.

Whichever staging-post was chosen, the Wellstream had to be forded to arrive in Wisbech, and it, too, was flanked by shifting sandbanks. This seems the most likely place for the disaster, but treasure-seekers still have to find the exact spot within an almost triangular area measuring some 10 miles from base to apex and some 5 miles across at the widest point. It has defeated them for seven centuries, and becomes harder as the land is developed and increasingly built up.

Legend says that one item of the treasure was salvaged, and it is on display in the Guildhall of the Holy Trinity in King's Lynn. The richly gilded, embossed and enameled vessel is known as King John's Cup. In its own right, it is a priceless example of medieval craftsmanship, but the style and content of the enameled panels show that it was made between 70 and 150 years after John's death.

The Whites in retreat

Above:
Alexander Vasilyevich Kolchak (1874-1920) commanded Russia's Black Sea fleet during World War I. Small, birdlike and a cocaine-user, he had a reputation for bravery and efficiency, as well as for a fiery temper. In 1918, he was nominated Supreme Ruler of All the Russias, at the head of the White forces.

Top right:
Heavily-armored trains called *broneviki*, lumbering along the Trans-Siberian Railroad at 15 mph, played a major part in the Russian Civil War. This one, the Orlik, belonged to the Czech Legion, who allied themselves with the anti-Bolshevik White Army. The Czechs escorted Admiral Kolchak, and the Whites' treasure, on the retreat from Omsk towards Irkutsk.

By November 1919, the Russian Civil War was two years old. The Red Army, welded by Leon Trotsky into a formidable fighting force, was advancing, while Admiral Kolchak's Whites, supported by the major Western powers, were in retreat eastwards along the Trans-Siberian Railroad from Omsk, their headquarters for the past year or so. With them, it is said, went a special train carrying the treasure, including a claimed 500 tons of gold (there must be considerable doubt whether that amount of bullion could even be moved by one train in those conditions).

Lost gold
Within a couple of months, Kolchak's reign was over. The Western allies had begun to court the Bolshevik government. Irkutsk, the central Siberian city earmarked as the Whites' next headquarters, had fallen to Bolshevik sympathizers. Kolchak had no choice but to surrender, yielding his mantle as 'supreme ruler' to General Denikin, who was still fighting the Reds in the south. Kolchak was tortured for several weeks, and finally shot, with many of his followers. Others managed to escape, but most froze to death trying to reach freedom. The gold, meanwhile, had disappeared somewhere in the 2,000 miles of Siberia between Omsk and Irkutsk.

Or so, at least, the story runs. As with the fate of the Tsar, there are many versions of what happened next. One is that the gold was not lost at all, but simply handed over to the Bolsheviks at Irkutsk by members of the Czech Legion that had associated itself with Kolchak, in return for their release. If that were the case, or if the Bolsheviks had found the gold in some hiding-place, they were under no obligation to publicize the fact, and may well have chosen not to do so.

On the other hand, rumor and tradition hold that the Bolsheviks did not obtain the treasure. Some argue that the remnants of the White Army kept it, and tried to move it across the frozen waters of Lake Baikal, near Irkutsk, the deepest lake in the world; when the ice melted, it plunged into the depths below. Others say it was hidden somewhere along the Trans-Siberian Railroad, in a disused mine or in the crypt of a ruined church, where it was stacked by soldiers who were subsequently shot to preserve the secret.

An alleged survivor of this incident, one Slava Bogdanov, reportedly returned to the site in 1959 with an American accomplice, and removed ingots weighing 325 pounds. Bogdanov was killed by frontier guards trying to crash a roadblock, and his haul was seized, it is claimed, leaving the unknown American the sole person with knowledge of the cache. This part of the quest ends in a seemingly blank wall.

However, there remains the third portion of the treasure. While Kolchak was threatening the Bolsheviks from the east, Denikin was harassing them from the south. He, too, had need of a war-chest, and may even at some stage have been given part of the imperial riches for that purpose. Certainly, he would have taken anything he could get from banks and abandoned private estates to pay his troops, buy weapons, and foment subversion.

A Black Sea cache

In 1973, in a book published in Paris, a Russian emigré, Nicholas Svidine, claiming to have served in Denikin's army, recounted events in southern Russia during the closing days of the Civil War in 1920 (that is when the Soviet Union says it finished; hostilities actually continued in Siberia for another two years). According to Svidine, Denikin realized defeat was imminent and ordered treasure to be amassed to finance continuing guerrilla resistance or an eventual reinvasion of Russia. The booty was assembled and somehow transferred to Bulgaria, which was along the Black Sea coast and became the destination for many fleeing Whites.

There it was temporarily concealed in a cellar before being divided into four caches and buried somewhere in wild woodland in the region of Bourgas, a major Black Sea port. So far as is known, it could still be hidden beneath the trees.

By all accounts, Denikin's treasure was not so impressive as that of Kolchak and was worth only about one-tenth as much – $100 million. Still, it represents a tidy fortune in thousands of gold roubles, foreign notes and coins, 450 pounds of platinum, baskets of cut and uncut gems, and stock certificates. In addition, there are said to be state documents revealing hitherto unknown facts about events during the Revolution and the Civil War; it is tempting to speculate that, if these papers really exist, they could contain clues to Kolchak's gold and the mystery of the imperial family.

Svidine apparently made efforts to relocate and remove the treasure, but without success. Bulgaria, since World War II a Soviet satellite, is unlikely to welcome foreign treasure-hunters. So perhaps we will never know what the documents contain – a secret almost as alluring as the four caches themselves.

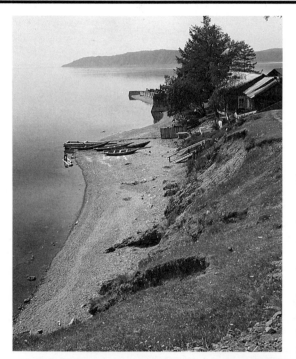

Left:
Lake Baikal, in the heart of Siberia, lay on the Whites' line of retreat from Omsk. Its deep waters may conceal Tsarist bullion, although other accounts suggest the gold might have been hidden somewhere near its shores. Certainly, many fleeing Whites drowned in the lake.

Below:
Two members of the Czech Legion guard freight cars at Kurgan, west of Omsk on the Trans-Siberian Railroad. Some 50,000 Czechs were in Russian territory in 1918, fighting the Austro-Hungarian Empire for the independence of their homeland. After World War I officially ended, the Czech Legion was virtually forced to join the Whites to try to obtain its passage home.

When the Romans withdrew

At the end of the 4th century AD, the western Roman Empire was beginning to crumble under the combined weight of barbarian onslaughts and internal dissension. Troops from far-flung outposts were recalled to help man frontiers nearer to Rome. In Britain, the imperial forces departed in AD 407, leaving the country vulnerable to Saxons from across the North Sea, who had been eyeing it greedily, and periodically raiding it, for several decades.

By about 600, the Saxons had conquered and settled much of present-day England and lowland Scotland, despite resistance by Romano-British leaders of whom the legendary Arthur was almost certainly one. But in the early days of the Saxon raids it was by no means apparent that Britain would be overrun. The Romano-British in the most vulnerable areas fled from their town-houses, villas, and farms – some to the fastnesses of Wales and the West Country. Often, they concealed those treasures they could not carry with them, fully intending to reclaim them later when the Saxon threat had been dealt with.

A pattern of concealment

From sites in Britain and elsewhere in Europe, we know these caches followed a pattern. In general, they were made at some distance from the buildings where the valuables originated, presumably to make them harder for the invaders to find; burial in the ground seems to have been the preferred method of concealment. At two of the richest British villas dating from this period – Lullingstone in Kent and Chedworth in Gloucestershire – no gold or silver items have been found, although there are lavish mosaics and murals, and plenty of semi-precious and everyday objects. On the other hand, a hoard of 4th-century silverware discovered at Water Newton in East Anglia is not associated with any building of the period in the immediate vicinity. So unearthing Roman treasure hidden from the barbarians is largely a matter of luck.

Certainly, luck played a large part in the discovery of the most important collection of Roman works of art yet found in Britain. It breaks our general rule, in that part of the site was no more than 30 yards from a 4th-century building, but there is no obvious link to connect that with the treasure.

A plowman's fortune

In 1942, a plowman working in the fields near Mildenhall in Suffolk decided, for reasons unclear to us, to set his plowshare deeper than usual. As the plow broke soil that had probably been untouched for centuries, it turned up an assortment of encrusted objects that appeared, when some of the earth was knocked away, to be lead or pewter, and therefore of little intrinsic value. The plowman handed these objects over to his employer, who took them home and thought little more about the matter.

But in 1946, the discovery was officially reported, and the objects were properly cleaned. The Mildenhall Treasure was revealed in all its magnificence – 34 pieces of priceless decorated silverware, of fine quality and almost perfectly preserved. Most date from the 4th century, but some are almost 200 years older, perhaps family heirlooms handed down through the generations. The majority came from Rome or Gaul, with a few that could be of local British manufacture.

There are goblets, dishes, and spoons, but two items in particular stand out. One is a silver salver 2 feet (60cm) in diameter and richly decorated with gods and monsters surrounding a centerpiece depicting Oceanus, god of the sea. The other is a bowl with a domed lid that shows centaurs, gods, and wild animals, topped with a knob in the shape of a Triton, another sea-deity, blowing a conch-shell horn.

The presumption is that the Mildenhall Treasure was buried by a well-to-do family to keep it from the Saxons and that, as well as being wealthy, the owners were probably well traveled because of the diverse origins of the pieces. Possibly it could have belonged to the general Lupicinus, whom the Emperor Julian sent to Britain in the 4th century to try to stem the barbarian invasions. Lupicinus was a Christian, and some of the spoons in the collection are of a type sometimes given as christening presents, although that of itself proves little. Julian, on the other hand, was the man who tried to turn the Roman Empire back to paganism. Eventually he had Lupicinus arrested, which perhaps was the reason the general never reclaimed his heirlooms.

Far right:
The most spectacular hoard of Roman silver ever found in Britain was unearthed at Mildenhall in Suffolk by a farmworker, Gordon Butcher, during World War II. The area, which is a rich source of Roman artifacts, was constantly threatened by Saxon raids from across the English Channel at the end of the 4th century AD, and it is assumed that the treasure was deliberately buried to conceal it from the raiders. The huge silver salver is the most striking of the 34 items in the collection, but all display exquisite craftsmanship. The treasure is now in the British Museum in London.

Emin Pasha's ivory

For centuries, two of the most valuable commodities in Saharan and sub-Saharan Africa were black and white 'gold' – slaves and ivory respectively. Both played a part in the primitive economy of Equatoria, the area broadly corresponding to today's southern Sudan.

In 1869, the ruler of Egypt, Khedive Ismail, appointed a Briton, Samuel Baker, to annex Equatoria and to stop the slave trade there. Four years later, the bushy-bearded, piratical Baker was succeeded as governor of the province by another Briton, General Charles Gordon, known as 'Chinese' Gordon from his previous military exploits in the Far East.

An ivory hoard

The ascetic, unmarried Gordon continued Baker's fight against the slavers, and succeeded in one area in which his predecessor had failed by persuading the natives to sell their ivory only to the Egyptian government. This monopoly produced the circumstances in which one of Africa's great lost-treasure mysteries was created.

Gordon rose to become governor-general of the whole Sudan, while his place in Equatoria was taken by the German-born Emin Pasha. But by 1881, the Sudan was torn by a revolt led by the Mahdi (the name means 'divine guide'), one Mohammed Ahmed, who wanted a return to the traditional ways of Islam and to drive out all the foreigners. In 1885, the Sudanese capital of Khartoum fell to the Mahdi's forces, and Gordon, who had been leading the defense, was killed.

The Mahdi's victory opened the rebels' way into Equatoria, where Emin Pasha remained with some loyal troops and about 200 tons of ivory he had collected but had been unable, because of the rebellion, to ship down the Nile. As the Mahdi's forces advanced, Emin retreated south, making caches of some of the precious elephant tusks and taking the rest with him to his new base at Wadelai.

Stanley to the rescue

Public opinion in Europe, aroused against the Mahdi by the siege of Khartoum and Gordon's death, demanded that something should be done to save Emin. In 1887, the veteran African explorer H M Stanley, who had previously gained fame by finding Dr David Livingstone, led a relief expedition. The expedition was beset by disasters – attacked by natives and disease, short of food, and without the promised support of 600 bearers. Eventually, Stanley and

Above:
After months of hardship, Stanley finally reached Emin Pasha near Lake Albert in what is now Zaire. But Emin (left) was not keen to leave his hoard of ivory, and only reluctantly agreed to make for Zanzibar. Much of the ivory is still buried somewhere in the area.

Left:
King Leopold II of Belgium sponsored H M Stanley's expedition to relieve the beleaguered Emin Pasha. In 1887, Stanley sailed up the River Congo and then trekked into the thick rain-forest, where ambushes by pygmies and disease lost him 200 men.

Below:
Two vessels used in the early stages of Stanley's rescue mission lie moored on the River Aruwhimi, a tributary of the Congo (now the River Zaire), about a mile below Stanley's base camp at Yambuya. The camp was left in the charge of Stanley's associate, Edmund Barttelot, who was murdered while Stanley made his first foray into the rain-forest.

his much-depleted band reached Emin Pasha, only to find that the governor did not wish to leave.

After months of argument and cajolery, Emin was finally persuaded he would be wiser to make for Zanzibar, on the East African coast, rather than remain where he was. The party was too small to carry more than a fraction of the ivory Emin still had with him, so a final cache was made somewhere near Lake Albert, on the borders of what are now Uganda and Zaire.

The choice of the site was carefully calculated, for it lay in a region to which Germany had claim; Emin felt that the tusks could be reclaimed later on behalf of his native land. However, the plan went sadly astray; the territory in question was eventually ceded to Britain.

Neither Emin nor Stanley managed to get back to the hoard. Emin was murdered in 1892 by the very slave-traders he, Gordon, and Baker had struggled against. So far as we know, he did not tell anyone of the exact location. Stanley did not die until 1904, but he never returned to Africa, and it is not clear whether or not he knew more than the approximate area in which the ivory was hidden.

Loot of the Axis

Right:
Hitler (left) shakes hands with Field Marshal Rommel during their meeting in October 1942 – a turning-point in the history of Germany's Third Reich. Within days, Rommel's North African troops were to be defeated at El Alamein, and within months Rommel would be forced to flee Africa altogether with the treasure he had accumulated.

Far right:
The Eagle's Nest, Hitler's mountain hideaway near Berchtesgaden in the Bavarian Alps, was to be the command-post for the Nazis' last stand during the final stages of World War II. Extensive preparations were made for defending it, but Hitler died in Berlin without retreating there. However, trainloads of Nazi treasure were moved to the area in the spring of 1945, including, it is said, vast quantities of gold bullion that have never been traced.

As the Nazis invaded much of Europe in the years between 1938 and 1943, the generals looted occupied territories in a manner unprecedented in scale and organization. Public and private art galleries and museums in France, Holland, Belgium, Czechoslovakia, Poland, Hungary, and elsewhere were stripped of their glories. Churches were ransacked, and bank vaults pillaged for coin and bullion. Millions of private citizens were forced to give up jewelry, family heirlooms, and other valuables under threat of torture.

No one can ever estimate the true worth of the treasures seized by the Third Reich and its allies, officially and unofficially. It certainly ran into billions of dollars, possibly trillions. Some of the works of art stolen were unique, and priceless.

Reclaiming the loot
The process of restoring this vast booty to its rightful owners began shortly after Germany surrendered in 1945, and is continuing even now. In the 1980s, for example, looted paintings were found in the home of a former Nazi official who had lived undetected for years under a false name.

According to official estimates, about 80 percent of the treasures plundered by the Nazis and their henchmen have been recovered. If one accepts that view, the value of the missing

portion is still astronomical. In fact, the estimate is wildly overoptimistic; it applies only to those items known to have been stolen – that is, of which there is some record. Millions of dollars in personal valuables alone are still missing.

Of the items officially stated to have disappeared, the bulk are either hidden or in private hands. In the chaos following the collapse of the Third Reich, many were looted by private individuals of both German and occupying forces, either for themselves or for sale on the black market. As the Allied powers entered Berlin, for example, securities worth $400 million were removed from the state bank, and the fate of only a fraction of this has been satisfactorily established. At the same time, bullion, coins, and jewels worth $200 million today disappeared without trace. A joint coup by German and American soldiers is usually offered as the explanation, but no one has ever been charged with this crime.

Booty at Berchtesgaden?
Inevitably, the most persistent rumors of lost treasures from World War II attach themselves to the leaders of the Axis powers – Hitler and the Italian dictator Benito Mussolini as well as many of the military commanders, including Field Marshal Erwin Rommel. One could fill a book with tales of Hitler's treasure which, according to preference, lies at the bottom of a

mountain lake on the German-Austrian border, or in a cave or disused mine nearby, or has been removed to South America by ex-Nazis or neo-Nazis working for the resurgence of a nationalistic and militaristic Germany. Like all theories of this type, there is probably more than a grain of truth behind it. Before his suicide in Berlin, Hitler had been planning to continue resistance against the invading Allies from his 'final redoubt', high in the mountains of southeastern Bavaria near Berchtesgaden and the Austrian city of Salzburg. Preparations for this last stand were well advanced in the spring of 1945, and it would have been natural to include in the materials destined for Berchtesgaden bullion and coin to pay loyal troops and to buy necessary armaments.

The theory is widely believed in Germany and Austria, particularly in the regions close to Berchtesgaden, where the inhabitants speak of Nazis burying large quantities of gold in the closing stages of the war. The details are blurred; the area offers deep lakes and disused saltmines as possible hiding-places, as well as large tracts of forest.

It was in the forests above Salzburg that a series of bizarre incidents occurred in the 1950s, possibly adding credibility to local rumors. In 1955, the body of a young man was found, dead from a bullet-wound between the eyes. Suicide was ruled out, because the bullet did not match the gun found by the victim's body, but there were no clues as to the perpetrator or the motive. Shortly afterwards, two climbers were stabbed to death nearby; close to their corpses were several holes in the ground, as though buried chests or boxes had been removed.

That would suggest that Hitler's treasure is now elsewhere. It may even have been smuggled to South America, the refuge of some prominent ex-Nazis. But there are many who believe it is still somewhere near Berchtesgaden, watched over by those who consider themselves Hitler's heirs and successors.

Rommel's treasure

By comparison with Hitler's reputed hoard, the fate of the treasure amassed by Field Marshal Rommel, the brilliant strategist who masterminded Germany's North Africa campaign, seems relatively straightforward, although it, too, has never to public knowledge been found.

Between March 1941 and October 1942, Rommel's Afrika Korps seemed unstoppable, driving back the Allies' desert forces and gaining control over Libya, much of Tunisia, and part of northern Egypt. In his triumphant progress, Rommel collected a large amount of gold, jewelry, works of art, and ivory, destined ultimately to swell the coffers of the Third Reich.

However, the tide of battle turned at El Alamein on 23rd October 1942, and by May of the following year most of North Africa was back in Allied hands. The Afrika Korps had been forced to retreat, taking the treasure with it, and Rommel escaped back to Europe. According to most accounts, his booty was flown to the island of Corsica days before the Allies could enforce an air and sea blockade, and stored there under German military control.

Booty in the Gulf of Bastia

But with the Allies preparing to invade Italy, there was little prospect of getting the treasure off the island. Measures were probably taken to hide it to prevent its falling into enemy hands. At any rate, at some stage in the fall of 1943, it disappeared. The most plausible version of events says that the spoils were taken aboard a German ship on the night of 18th September 1943, and dumped at sea in the Gulf of Bastia, at the northeastern corner of Corsica opposite the Isle of Elba. Many attempts have been made to locate it there, including one in the 1960s involving an ex-soldier who claimed to have taken part in the dumping and therefore to know the precise spot.

He was convincing enough to persuade backers to set up a consortium and dive for the treasure. However, before the salvage

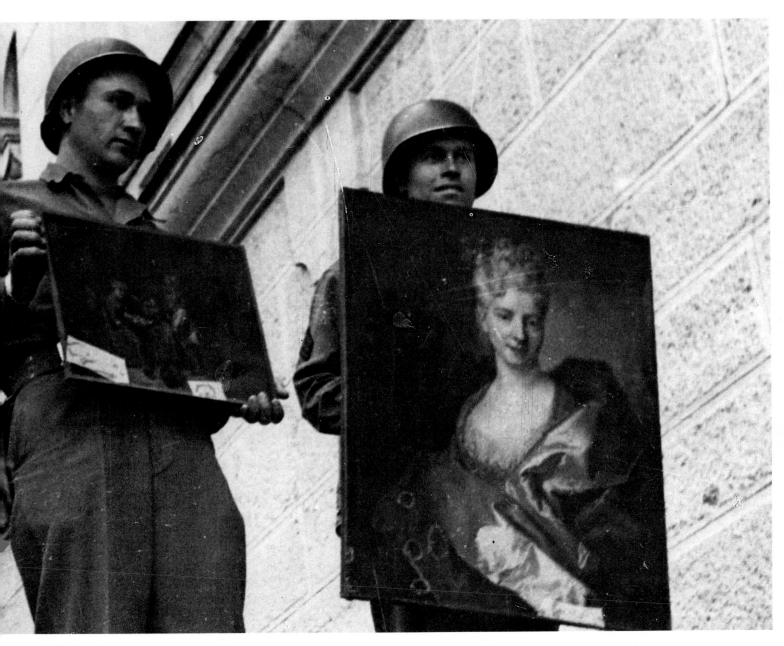

operation could start, the ex-soldier suffered a sudden loss of memory and could no longer identify the location, so the expedition was called off. Shortly afterwards, the would-be guide disappeared – killed, say some, by the same ring of ex-Nazis allegedly watching over Hitler's hoard.

The mystery of Mussolini's millions

By contrast, no self-appointed band of guardians is reputedly preserving another collection of water-entrusted war-spoils – the personal fortune of Italy's fascist leader, Mussolini. He was overthrown by his own people a bare two months before Rommel's treasure vanished, but escaped to the north of Italy with the aid of the Germans, who then set him up as a puppet ruler of the so-called Republic of Salò.

Early in 1945, it became clear that the Germans could no longer resist the Allied forces moving inexorably up the Italian boot. They, and Mussolini, fled. The former dictator and his mistress, Claretta Petacci, got as far as Lake Como, where they were recognized, captured, and shot by partisans, and their bodies hanged upside-down on public display.

Otto Kisnatt, leader of Mussolini's German guards, was luckier, managing to escape and survive the war. According to him, he did so carrying two large suitcases stuffed with jewels, which he threw into Lake Como.

Kisnatt kept the story to himself until 1957, when he told it to the German and Italian police. An official search was immediately organized, but nothing was found of the suitcases, which may still lie somewhere at the bottom of the lake.

Above:
Neuschwanstein Castle at Füssen, near the Austrian frontier, was another of the many repositories for treasures pillaged by the Nazis from all over Europe. When the US 7th Army uncovered the Neuschwanstein hoard in 1945, few of the valuable paintings had even been removed from their packing-cases. Hitler was to have first pick of the plunder, and the remainder was destined for the Hermann Goering Gallery, to be built at Linz in Austria.

Chapter 6

The Proceeds of Crime

It has been argued that those who today choose to live outside the law have never had it so good – or so easy. With modern high-tech hard and software to aid them, ranging from computers to lasers, and plastic surgery to ultrasound, they would seem to have everything on their side. But it should be remembered that law enforcement officers also have access to these very handy helps, and they are usually better organized and better funded.

And down through the centuries the problem has not been so much one of getting hold of the loot as *getting rid of it.* Highwaymen, hijackers, outlaws, and city slickers alike have all had to face this problem, and in their efforts to solve it have often left behind them sizable caches which still await discovery. Here are some of the stories of just such proceeds of crime, and how they came to be hidden.

An enormous haul of loot went missing from a French bank in July 1976. Valued at between $8 and $10 million, it was one of the boldest, most successful, and most insolent of all robberies, and the proceeds are still being sought.

Underground vaults

Ex-paratrooper and professional thief, 45-year-old Albert Spaggiari with nine accomplices broke into a branch of the Société Générale in Nice on 16th July. They tunneled into an underground vault, then spent 48 undisturbed hours rifling through more than 400 safety deposit boxes at leisure. While they removed jewelry, securities, bonds, and cash, they fortified themselves with ample food and wine

which they had taken in with them. Among their finds were a number of pornographic pictures which some depositor had allegedly kept there for possible blackmail purposes. The robbers grabbed these and plastered them all round the walls of the strongroom!

Early in 1977 Spaggiari was caught and brought to trial. He promised the judge that he would hand over detailed plans of how the robbery was carried out. But this magnanimous gesture *was* only a gesture. There was a brief scuffle in the courtroom and Spaggiari had broken free from his guards. Using his paratroop training to good effect, he leapt out of the second-story window to land unharmed on the roof of a waiting car parked below. The car disappeared at high speed, and neither the loot nor Spaggiari have been seen since.

There are numerous instances of robberies having been committed with the villains brought to trial or otherwise disposed of before all of the proceeds were recovered. As a result, much loot still lies hidden, waiting for some lucky passerby to stumble upon it. Just such a situation arose from the holdup of the Deadwood Stage in 1878.

Deadwood gold

Two years before that, gold had been discovered in the Black Hills of South Dakota. Consignments were regularly transported from Deadwood, a typically lawless mining town, via the Cheyenne and Black Hills Stage Line to Cheyenne, the Wyoming capital. This particular line used an armored coach, named *Monitor,* to carry valuable cargo, and it had an enviable record of success in its operations.

An ex-soldier called Charles Carey, who had battled against Indians with Custer, cared nothing for the *Monitor*'s reputation and, tempted by the $400,000 in bullion that the stage usually carried, decided to help himself to some of it. Accordingly, on 26th September, he and his men laid an ambush at the Canyon Springs stage post, not far from Deadwood. After overpowering the stable hand and locking him in the grain store, he dispersed his band among the surrounding barns and stables.

The *Monitor* rolled into Canyon Springs on time as usual, and stopped to change its team of six horses. Carey and his men immediately opened fire, killing a telegraph operator and wounding two of the guards. But before the stage surrendered, one of the guards and the stable hand managed to escape and raise the alarm. They also slew two of Carey's gang.

Carey was then faced with the problem of opening a huge, securely locked, iron and steel chest. He knew that a posse from Deadwood would soon be on their heels, so speed was essential. Nevertheless, it took them all of two hours to smash open the chest with sledgehammers, crowbars, and chisels. They discovered diamonds, jewelry, $3,500 in cash, and 700 pounds of gold bars.

Because they had to make a quick getaway, Carey buried much of the heavy gold in two caches – one at Canyon Springs and the other at Pino Springs. It was only a matter of time before all the bandits were caught. Carey himself fell into the hands of vigilantes and was promptly strung up by them. Only a little more

than half the loot was ever recovered, and the cache at Canyon Springs remains hidden to this day.

Sometimes the proceeds from a potentially huge haul are dissipated by the perpetrators in a getaway attempt. Substantial sums are paid out for safe houses, plastic surgery, false passports, and the like, and at the end of it all, the miserable fugitive is lucky if he can survive without having to work for a living once more. Money disappeared fast in this way after what was billed as the crime of the century in England: The Great Train Robbery.

Great train robbery

It took place in 1963, on the evening of 7th August. The Royal Mail Train (in reality a traveling post office) left Glasgow, Scotland, on its way to Euston Station in London, where it would arrive the following morning. Right at the front of the train was a special van holding 120 bags. Each bag was stuffed with used and grubby one-pound and five-pound bills. At three in the morning, about 36 miles from London on a lonely stretch of track, the driver stopped for a red signal.

Masked men, armed with iron bars, axes, and other weapons, suddenly rushed the train and overpowered the driver and guard. They uncoupled the locomotive and the van with the money in it, leaving the rest of the train stationary on the track, with the postal sorters busily working and blissfully unaware of what had happened. They broke into the high-value van after pulling it half a mile down the track to where a convenient bridge carried the getaway

Above:
In this raid on a branch of the American Security and Trust Company in Washington, DC, three armed men burst into the building while a fourth man waited in a car outside. In the background one of the robbers holds his gun to the head of a guard; a second man aims his gun at the staff; and a third clambers over the counter to get at the money. In spite of all three being caught on film by the bank's hidden camera, the robbers got away with more than $10,000.

cars and trucks.

The workers inside that van quickly surrendered when faced with the masked gang, and within half an hour $6 million (£2.6 million) had been transferred to a temporary hideout. This was a recently rented farmhouse, Leatherslade Farm, in deserted countryside near Oakley, in Buckinghamshire. It was some 18 miles from the scene of the holdup.

There were allegedly 17 robbers in all. If so, three of them have never been traced. Seven men were the big fish. They had planned everything in meticulous detail, including faking the signals to stop the train originally and cutting the emergency telephone wires by the track. But when the seven came to divide the spoils in the farmhouse, they grew careless and left fingerprints all over the place.

In spite of the fact that the crooks had at least an hour's start, the police were soon on their trail. The seven were all eventually rounded up, tried, convicted and sentenced to an astonishing term (in England) of 30 years each in jail. This was later reduced on appeal.

Each of the top men took about $360,000 out of the kitty. As the police closed in, some of the robbers began to lose their nerve and looked for places to hide the cash that weighed so heavily on them. Some $45,000 was found in a little Surrey town called East Molesey. A car and a truck in London concealed a quarter of a million dollars. A similar sum turned up in a forest near Dorking, and $70,000 lay in an abandoned caravan.

Only two men managed to hold on to their share of the loot. Douglas Gordon Goody salted his $360,000 away so well that it presumably awaited him after he had served his time. Ronald Arthur Biggs, the most notorious of the gang, escaped from jail after 12 months. He fled first to Australia and then to Rio, where, in the mid-1980s, he was still living. But all his money had been spent in high-priced bribes to ensure his safe flight halfway across the world. In Brazil he was reduced to simple carpentering jobs and expensive interviews in order to make ends meet in quite spartan surroundings.

As for the rest of the haul? Well, about $5 million is still missing, perhaps scattered somewhere along England's green and leafy lanes.

Sometimes the proceeds of a criminal haul can never be recovered. Such a situation arose in part after the theft of the Crown Jewels of Hesse-Darmstadt, one of the great old aristocratic families of Europe.

U.S. find

Toward the end of World War II, the Grand Duchess Margarethe of Hesse had moved out of her home, Kronberg Castle, in the Taunus Mountains, in Germany, and had given it up to General Patton's advancing armies. But before that, she had hidden the crown jewels under a stone slab in the cellar, for safekeeping until after the war.

During her absence the box had been found by some American soldiers, forced open, and apparently handed over to some officers. Early in 1946, Princess Sophie of Hesse was about to get married to Prince Georg Wilhelm of Hanover. She thought she would like to wear some of the crown jewels (a family heirloom) at her wedding, so she went to the Americans who were still occupying the castle and asked them to return the jewels.

This was the first the Americans had heard of the affair. Subsequent inquiries showed that among the residents at the castle at the time that the jewels went missing was a welfare officer, Captain Kathleen B Nash, and a Colonel James W Durant. These two had married soon after their return to the States. During a routine check by investigators, the Durants began to run. They were arrested, and eventually the

true story came out.

The soldiers who found the crown jewels apparently took them to Miss Nash, who then showed them to Durant. The two of them, together with a Major Watson, decided to take the jewels, sell them, and start a business on the proceeds. After questioning, Durant took his interrogators to a rented locker in the Chicago station of the Illinois Central Railroad. There, in a cardboard box, lay a heap of gleaming jewels, prised from their costly settings.

More of the royal regalia was found at the home of Mrs Durant's sister. This good lady had accepted as a gift from Kathleen Durant a solid gold dinner service studded with gems. Unaware of its value and historic associations, she had kept it for everyday use! Up to that time, the investigators had recovered about half a million dollars' worth of the treasure.

Bracelets and tiaras

Major David F Watson was the next to be located, still serving in Germany. After spending some time with him the investigators were able to lay their hands on more of the loot: diamond bracelets, pearl tiaras, and amethyst rings. Some of the original settings also turned up in a goldsmith's shop in Belfast, Northern Ireland.

All these items were proudly returned to the Grand Duchess in Frankfurt, but she was adamant that many items were still missing. While the army agents resumed their search, Mrs Durant was tried, found guilty of theft, and sentenced to five years in jail and dishonorable discharge from the army. Watson was also found guilty, and was given three years and a dishonorable discharge. Durant, the alleged mastermind behind the conspiracy, got 15 years' hard labor and was dismissed from the army.

Shortly before Durant's trial, three quart pickle jars had been found buried by a roadside in Durant's home state of Virginia. Two held jewels wrenched from the royal regalia, the third was stuffed with cash to the tune of some $15,000. Later, more jewels were discovered in the walls of a cottage in the grounds of Kronberg Castle.

And that was just about the final tally. Much of the regalia, according to Prince Philip of Hesse, is still missing and unaccounted for. It will probably never be recovered because the missing gems will no doubt have been cut and reshaped to make them unidentifiable and salable on the international market.

Another crown jewel robbery ended on a happier note. This involved the English crown jewels and took place centuries ago.

The crown jewels had originally been stolen by Oliver Cromwell in 1649. They were recovered and returned to the Tower of London under heavy armed guard. There lived at that

Top far left:
Great Train Robber Ronald Biggs, the one that got away, poses bronzed and relaxed in sunny Rio de Janeiro. His young son Mike, who saved him from deportation to England, points gleefully to a picture of his father taken at his arrest for the robbery in 1963. Father and son were celebrating the 20th anniversary of his escape from an English prison. Allegedly, most of Biggs' share of the loot went on paying for that escape.

Far left:
The so-called British Great Train Robbery of 1963 is the largest recorded train robbery of all time. The bandits got away with 120 mailbags stuffed with about £2,632,000 ($6 million) in used bills. Nearly all the robbers were eventually caught, but only £343,448 ($800,000) was ever recovered. The picture shows a man of average height standing beside the mountainous stack of bills that would have made up the huge haul.

time, in an apartment above the jewel room in Martin Tower (part of the Tower of London), a man and wife called Talbot and Dolly Edwardes. Their job was to clean the jewels and help guard them. They also served as guides, greeting distinguished visitors who had permission to view the jewels. The Edwardes would then explain their origin and history.

In April 1671 the caretakers were visited by a clergyman and his wife. They paid several visits to the Tower and eventually struck up a social friendship with the Edwardes. On one of these visits the minister confided that he was acquainted with a rich young man who would make an ideal match for the Edwardes' daughter, and he arranged to bring the gentleman with him on his next visit so that the prospective parents-in-law could give him the once-over.

Jewel thieves

On 9th May the clergyman returned with not one but two men, one he called his nephew, the other, the alleged suitor. The minister suggested that Edwardes might care to show his friends round the jewel room. Edwardes complied, but as soon as they entered the room, the three men knocked him down, and bound and gagged him. They then set about the jewels.

The minister flattened the crown with a mallet, in order to slip it into his pocket. The second man grabbed hold of the golden ball of the royal orb. The third man filed the scepter in half and put one half in each of two specially made pockets. As they were leaving the Tower the guards spotted them and raised the alarm. Within an hour the treasure had been recovered.

The fake parson turned out to be the notorious Colonel Thomas Blood, an Irish rebel who had fought with Cromwell and who had already attempted several times to kidnap the royal family. At his trial, Blood refused to answer questions unless they were put to him directly by the king himself. Charles II was so intrigued by this reply that he insisted on visiting the prisoner. During the ensuing conversation the monarch was so impressed and amused that he reprieved Blood from his mandatory death sentence. He also restored his estate and granted him an annual pension of £300.

Colonel Blood was no doubt grateful for large mercies but saw no reason to change his ways. He continued to plot against the Crown until his death in 1680.

Far left:
During a robbery at the Lee-Harvard branch of the National City Bank in Cleveland, Ohio, one of the gunmen noticed the camera and vented his annoyance by pumping lead into it from close range. The haul amounted to $11,600, but as a result of pictures taken by the camera under fire, one man was later arrested and a suspect was identified.

Left:
A bank raid in London, England in 1981, being secretly filmed by a hidden TV camera. After £4,000 ($6,000) in cash was handed over by helpless staff, one of the three armed youths involved in the robbery incautiously pulled down his face mask, thus providing the police with an excellent mugshot.

Left:
Anxious clients line up in front of the closed gates of the Bank of the Société Générale in Nice, France, awaiting news of their savings. Robbers had broken into the underground vaults of the bank and had then spent several undisturbed hours picking at leisure through the contents of the safety deposit boxes to carry out one of the boldest crimes of the century.

Capone's concrete cashbox?

Above:
Al Capone (1899-1947) was undisputed king of America's underworld during the 1920s and 1930s. After a knife brawl that left him with an angry scar running from eye to lip down his cheek, he became known to the world as 'Scarface'. With his headquarters in Chicago, he climbed to the top in crime by eliminating rivals through intimidation, bribery and murder. After a seemingly charmed career of unremitting violence, he was finally jailed for tax offenses, and eventually died in obscurity of syphilis of the brain.

In the mid-1980s, workers demolishing an abandoned 10-story building were astonished to uncover a mysterious concrete vault which is believed to have been built on the orders of Al Capone. There was excited speculation about its contents, ranging from bodies, booze, a car, to substantial amounts of his ill-gotten and still missing gains, in cash, or gold, or both.

Al Capone was the infamous gangster who became a worldwide symbol of Prohibition crime in the 1920s and 30s. He built up an enormous and much-feared organization that had its fingers in many criminal pies, including bribery, prostitution, gambling, and, especially, illegal liquor sales. He organized the notorious St Valentine's Day massacre of 1929 when some of his gang mowed down eight rival gangsters with machine-guns. In spite of his murderous record, and a personal fortune built up from robbery and extortion that was estimated at more than $100 million, all the police could indict him for was income tax evasion. For this he was fined $70,000 and

jailed for 11 years in 1931. In 1939 he was released from Alcatraz, and survived semi-paralyzed until 1947.

The building where the vault was found was known to be Capone's Chicago headquarters during his heyday. The vault was located beneath the sidewalk in front of the old Lexington Hotel (a 400-room brothel in Capone's era) on Michigan Avenue. The vault itself is 125 feet long, 6 feet high, and 6 feet wide (38 × 1.8 × 1.8m). Preliminary external examination gave little away. Expert opinion was divided as to whether it was hollow. Those who believed it was, pointed out that there was absolutely no structural reason for a solid object of that nature being there. The vault at this date awaits X-ray investigation.

Interesting sidelights arose from renewed interest in the old gangster's elaborate hideaway. Chicago's central business district is apparently honeycombed with underground railroad tunnels. Originally they were used to facilitate the movement of coal to downtown stores and offices. Later, they housed steam pipes, and today fiber-optic cables are being laid along their length.

It appears that in the 1930s Capone employed an army of Italian immigrants to dig tunnels to link his headquarters with these railroad tunnels. As a result, he had access to key city offices, including city hall. The tunnels also provided handy escape routes, should he need them, and were used to carry loads of bootleg liquor to various parts of the city. The hotel itself was riddled with secret exits, and Capone once boasted that he could completely empty the hotel within a quarter of an hour without anybody ever having to use the streets. Capone reserved one entire floor for himself and ensconced his mistress comfortably on the floor above.

Rumors of vast wealth cached away somewhere in the building have persisted over the years since the gangster's death. Sewer workers have reported finding jewelry in the drains, including a diamond-and-sapphire stickpin and several gold coins. So what's in the vault? It's obviously anybody's guess, but an interesting clue has already surfaced. The Internal Revenue Service claims that Capone's estate is still in debt to the tune of more than $201,000, in addition to accrued interest. The first thing the IRS did when the vault was discovered was to slap an $800,000 lien on its contents. And they're no fools.

Above:
Federal agents proudly uncover a bootlegger's illicit liquor still during the Prohibition Era, before pouring away its contents into the sewers. By the late 1920s Al Capone had established a bootlegging empire that netted more than $100 million a year in profits. He got rid of all competition by corrupting the police, rigging elections and mass murder. The liquor, however, had quite nasty side effects — it contained poisons that could blind, paralyze, or kill, so earning its nicknames of 'rotgut' and 'coffin varnish'.

Big hoard on the Big Horn

Almost everybody has heard of Custer's Last Stand in the Battle of the Little Big Horn. What many don't realize is that at the time of the massacre, and in roughly the same area, a whole heap of gold went missing, and is still being sought today. The strange cycle of events was unearthed by American author Emile C Schumacher during some research into military history.

Crazy Horse
Three strands came together on that fateful day in 1876. The first consisted of Lieutenant-Colonel George Armstrong Custer, commanding the 7th Cavalry. He and his regiment were seeking to capture escaped Sioux and Cheyenne Indians in order to return them to their reservations. Custer was in Montana Territory at the time in a region bounded by the Big Horn, Little Big Horn, and Little Horn rivers. He came across an Indian camp in a valley along the Little Big Horn River. Believing that the camp held only about 1,000 Indians, and disdaining the offer of help and reinforcements from Brigadier-General Alfred Terry to the east, Custer hurled his force of 225 tired men into the attack. The camp contained at least 1,500 fighting men (some reports put the figure as high as 5,000) led by such legendary characters as Sitting Bull, Crazy Horse, and Gall. Within an hour, Custer's column was wiped out to a man.

The second strand in the saga was the riverboat *Far West,* hired by the US Cavalry to supply the troops with food and equipment. The *Far West,* skippered by 52-year-old Grant Marsh, drew less than two feet of water in ballast, and was ideal for navigating unknown waters. At the time of Custer's ill-timed foray, the riverboat was plying the Big Horn en route to a rendezvous with General Terry at the junction of the Big Horn and the Little Big Horn.

The third strand involved a mule-drawn freight wagon galloping along a dusty trail some 50 miles west of the Big Horn River. It had set out from Bozeman, Montana, and was headed for Bismark, North Dakota. On board were the driver, Gil Longworth, two men riding shotgun, Jergens and Dickson, and a shipment of miners' gold in dust and nuggets valued at about $50,000. Longworth and his two guards were distinctly unhappy. They had already survived a couple of attacks by marauding Indians and the remainder of the journey looked fraught.

Meanwhile, the *Far West* had missed the agreed rendezvous with General Terry by sailing past the confluence of the two rivers. Marsh was preparing to return downstream when he spotted Longworth and his wagon on the river bank. Longworth begged Marsh to relieve him of the gold because the area was crawling with hostile Indians. Marsh agreed, and the gold was hastily shipped aboard the *Far West*.

Later that evening, Marsh became aware of increasing Indian activity all around him and decided it would be prudent to hide the gold somewhere ashore and collect it later. Accordingly, Marsh himself, Foulk (his engineer) and Ben Thompson (his first mate) rowed ashore with the bags of gold and buried them.

Bullet-ridden
By this time Terry had joined battle with the Sioux and driven them off, only to discover the corpses of Custer and his men. He finally rendezvoused with the *Far West* and commandeered the boat to ferry his wounded troops to Bismark. Marsh was therefore unable to retrieve the gold. Gil Longworth failed to run the Indian gauntlet and his bullet-ridden body was discovered some days later.

In 1879 Marsh tried to trace Longworth's employers and the names of the owners of the gold, which had been sewn onto tabs on individual bags. But it was all in vain. Marsh, Thompson, and Foulk, the three men who knew exactly where the treasure was hidden, went on working for the rest of their lives with no signs of having acquired sudden significant wealth. The assumption must be, therefore, that the gold still lies where it was cached in 1876. It is known that the site lies some 15 to 20 miles up the Big Horn River from its junction with the Little Big Horn, on the west bank.

Canadian capers

For sheer boldness, ingenuity, and luck, the exploits of Georges Lemay, Canadian ex-seaman and fisherman, take some beating. Lemay first hit the headlines in 1952, after the mysterious disappearance of his young wife. He was strongly suspected of having murdered her, but none of the evidence could be made to stick.

Five years later, Lemay's name surfaced once more in suspicious circumstances, this time linked with the disappearance of one Larry Petrov. Petrov was a resident of Montreal who had been charged with narcotics offenses. The best the police could do this time was to arrest Lemay for carrying two unregistered firearms. After a brief spell in jail he again went to ground and was not heard of again until 1961.

On 1st July of that year a daring robbery was carried out on a Montreal branch of the Bank of Nova Scotia. Hundreds of deposit boxes were rifled of their contents and initial estimates of the haul in negotiable securities and jewels varied between half a million and four million dollars, making it the largest robbery in Canadian history. In the event, the final tally was computed at $633,605.

Dozens of suspects were rounded up, and after the usual period of grilling it was established that in this case Lemay was 'Mr Big', the mastermind behind the whole complex operation. He had apparently left nothing to chance, and after meticulous planning had put his gang through endless dress rehearsals, devising ingenious periods of practice with specialized equipment. During the actual robbery, Lemay had stationed himself outside in the street and directed operations with a walkie-talkie. One witness explained: 'Lemay called all the shots and never showed his face inside the bank until it was time to take the money from the vault.'

The hunt is on

After it was over, Lemay fled with almost all the money and jewelry and seemingly vanished from the face of the earth. He became the most hunted bank robber on four continents.

But the end was not yet. Some four years later, in May 1965, the Royal Canadian Mounted Police flashed a series of 'wanted' pictures of Lemay on an Early Bird satellite experimental TV program. A Florida boat-repair man who happened to be watching immediately recognized the mug shots as a man he knew as René Roy, whose 43-foot yacht was anchored at nearby Bahia Mar basin. Roy/Lemay had been living on the yacht for six months, paying his debts with wads of $100 bills.

The boatman tipped off the police, who quickly surrounded the yacht and captured Lemay without much trouble. The puzzled bandit couldn't understand how they had managed to trace him. After they had told him how, all he could say was, 'Well, isn't that something! It took a satellite to catch me!'

Once more in custody, Lemay managed to get himself married in one of history's fastest weddings. His bride this time was Lise Lemieux, a young blonde who in 1962 had been convicted of receiving some of the Montreal bank money. Lemay contrived to have the ceremony performed in an immigration office, just before his court hearing. This meant, in effect, that his new wife could not testify against him and was allowed to visit him regularly in prison. She probably helped also to plan and carry out his escape a few weeks later, which involved some $35,000 in prison bribes.

On 21st May Lemay managed to break out of his cell on the top floor of a maximum security prison. He took the elevator to the seventh floor, calmly stepped out of a window, climbed 90 feet (27m) down to the ground, and into a waiting car. It was nearly a year before Lemay was seen again.

On 1st August 1966 FBI agents in Las Vegas, Nevada, laid their hands on a certain Mr and Mrs Robert G Palmer, who turned out to be none other than our friend Lemay and Lise once more. They were carrying nearly $10,000 in US and Canadian currency. In 1968 Lemay was tried and sentenced to eight years in the penitentiary. He was released in 1975 and now lives in Montreal, free but apparently penniless. The original loot was never recovered.

Left:
Georges LeMay, 39-year-old fugitive Canadian bank robber, is arrested shirtless aboard a luxury yacht berthed near Fort Lauderdale, Florida, after four years on the run.

Pie in the sky

Above:
The audacious skyjacker who leaped out of a Northwest Airlines Boeing 727 in 1971, hugging a $200,000 ransom to his body, disappeared literally out of the blue. He called himself 'D B Cooper'. An artist's composite picture, released by the FBI and based on a description by fellow passengers, shows him as a swarthy middle-aged man with dark glasses.

Far right:
'D B Cooper' was unquestionably an experienced parachutist who knew what he was doing. In spite of being denied all the safety equipment he had demanded, and unlooked-for complications with the cash holdall, he timed his jump precisely. Some experts believe that he may have landed in a tiny wooded area east of Washington, but whether in one piece or not, we shall probably never know.

On 24th November 1971 a man leapt out of an airplane over the state of Washington clutching $200,000, and neither hide nor hair of him or the money has been seen since.

The story of the first skyjacker to parachute to earth with his loot (since dubbed 'parajacker') began when a man who gave his name as D B Cooper boarded a B-727 at Portland, Oregon. With hindsight, it is obvious that he was a skilled parachutist who chose his aircraft well. The B-727 has a tail-exit which would allow a jumper to keep clear of fuselage and engines.

Described as a tall, powerfully built man in his mid-forties, Cooper was wearing a black trenchcoat over a conventional outfit of coat and slacks. He hid only behind brown-tinted glasses, sat at the back of the plane, and spoke and acted quietly. During the flight he asked the air hostess to pass a note to the pilot in which he demanded $200,000 in $20 bills stacked in a knapsack, plus two backpack and two chestpack parachutes. To encourage the hostess, he opened his briefcase to reveal what looked like a number of sticks of dynamite wired together.

This was all to take place after the aircraft had

made its first stop at Seattle. Refueling there was deliberately slowed down, and for the first time Cooper began to lose his cool. Nor was he too pleased when the money he'd demanded was brought to him in a white cloth sack. This meant that he would now have to carry it instead of being able to sling it from his shoulders. The 10,000 $20 bills weighed a manageable 24 pounds, packed into a parcel measuring just 8 × 6 × 27 inches (20 × 15 × 70cm) – further evidence of Cooper's careful planning.

After taking off from Seattle, Cooper ordered pilot W Bill Scott to head for Mexico City via Reno, Nevada. He told him to fly at a steady height of 7,000 feet (2,100m), let down the landing gear, and use 15 percent flaps. As a result, the aircraft would be flying through the night at around 200 mph, thus enabling Cooper to calculate his position over a predetermined dropping zone with reasonable accuracy.

Soon after takeoff Cooper ordered the rear exit to be opened, and 32 minutes after departure from Seattle, at 2013 precisely, he baled out. He left two of the parachutes behind him on the aircraft. One had strips torn off it, which were presumably used to bind the money sack to his body. He jumped with just one serviceable backpack, because the other chestpack he took with him was intended for ground practice only, and was useless in the air.

There ensued an almost immediate and intensive search for the missing skyjacker and his loot. His landing zone, calculated by computer, seems to have been an area of about 15 square miles some 30 to 40 miles north of Portland. Right there Cooper would have landed in heavily wooded country at the foot of the Cascade Mountains.

Reaction to the exploit was often one of admiration. A devoted parajack cult built up on the West Coast, and graphic T-shirts inscribed D B Cooper – Where Are You? sold out rapidly. There was even a flattering record cut, which saturated the California airwaves with lyrics that referred to his 'dropout style'. A more serious consequence of Cooper's dramatic exit was the rash of imitators which it spawned. Within a year there had been a further 21 skyjack attempts, all demanding ransoms, but very few involving actual jumps.

As for Cooper himself, he is today either enjoying the fruits of his fall or – more likely – rotting in some hole in the ground with $200,000 scattered beside him, just waiting to be picked up.

The great Plymouth mail robbery

In the summer of 1962 in Cape Cod, Massachusetts, the cash tills never seemed to stop ringing as bronzed tourists readily parted with their greenbacks. This meant that the local banks were hard pressed to accommodate the overflow of money. As a result, vast quantities of cash had to be siphoned off regularly to the Federal Reserve Bank in Boston. The 75-mile journey along Route 3 was taken by ordinary mail trucks filled to capacity with canvas bags. The trucks were normally protected by state police, but that year the escort was withdrawn because it was considered unnecessary. Perhaps the US Post Office had full confidence in the driver and the guard of each truck, both armed.

Heading for trouble
On the evening of 14th August, there was a routine delivery of $1½ million in bills of small denomination to be made. Driver Patrick Schena, accompanied by his guard William Barrett, boarded the truck at Hyannis with cargo already aboard. The weather was fine with no sign of the trouble to come as they approached the town of Plymouth, the first sizable population center on their route.

The land near Plymouth is fairly hilly and in some places the center island between the two superhighways (as much as 100 yards apart) is so high that drivers in one lane cannot be seen from the other one. It was at such a spot, just past what is known as the Clark Road exit, that Schena and Barrett were overtaken by two speeding cars. As they glanced to the rear, they saw that Route 3, the route they were on, had suddenly sprouted a chain of detour signs, which meant that all northbound traffic behind them would be diverted through the exit. The Clark Road entrance had been blocked in the same way. The mail truck was completely cut off.

Schena and Barrett drove on warily and about two miles farther on, where the center island hid the view from the southbound highway, one of the speeding cars that had passed them earlier swung out from the side of the road broadside on. As the truck skidded to a halt, Barrett found himself staring into the barrel of a tommy gun wielded by a large gentleman in police uniform. His smaller mate introduced himself in similar fashion to Schena at the opposite window.

The driver and his guard were bundled into the back of the truck and forced to lie on the floor with their hands and feet tied. The phoney cop with the gun kept them company while his mate drove the truck. It stopped several times at unidentified places along a bumpy road, and each time some of the canvas bags were offloaded. Finally, with the truck empty save for its human cargo, the robbers decamped. Just before they went they warned the two prisoners to 'lie still for 15 minutes'.

Time to get out
When Schena and Barrett eventually freed themselves they found they were parked south of Boston, about 40 miles from where they had been hijacked. They were on a breakdown lane of Route 128, which rings Boston and links up with Route 3. The time was 9.35 pm, and $1,551,277 was missing.

The media seized on the story as the greatest heist ever on American soil. Rewards of all kinds were offered for the arrest and conviction of the bandits. The postal inspection service decided that this was their pigeon and took charge of the investigation. They arrested suspects, searched premises, announced that they had broken the case, and turned up with – nothing.

After several dead ends had been explored, the prime suspects were narrowed down to three: Jack Kelley, Tom Richards, and Mrs Patricia Diafario.

In 1967, five years after the robbery, the three of them were indicted to appear before a grand jury investigating the case. After a prolonged court wrangle they were all acquitted.

None of the missing money has ever been recovered.

Right:
Jack Kelley, of Watertown, Massachusetts, (here seen between two detectives) was arrested and charged with the robbery, along with three other suspects. The well-planned heist, which came to be known as the Plymouth Mail Robbery, was never solved, nor the money recovered. Kelley and others were hauled before a special grand jury, but partly because of inept procedures by post office officials, the defendants were eventually acquitted.

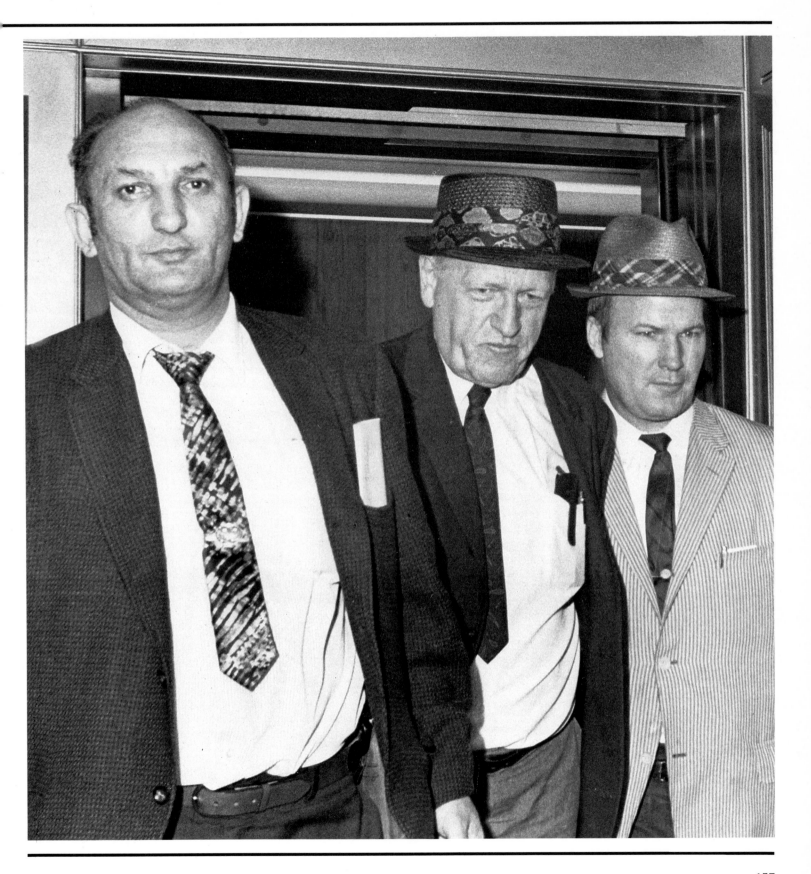

Chapter 7

Art Mysteries

The problem with works of art, unlike many of the treasures described in this book, is that their value depends entirely on their cultural significance as 'art'. Unlike, say, a hoard of gold coins or precious stones, they have no intrinsic value. As such, they have attracted the attention of the acquisitive down the ages, but for an unusual variety of reasons, and often with curiously double-edged results.

The appreciation of art as worthwhile treasure is largely the product of the enlightened attitude of the Renaissance. In Roman times conquering generals were expected to bring home large quantities of loot from their vanquished enemies, their success being judged by the number of slaves they captured or by the chests of gold coins they plundered, but these were largely practical benefits in the timeless tradition of sack and pillage. The slaves were a useful addition to the workforce, and the gold offset the cost of the expedition. Articles of artistic merit were of no significance unless they had a strictly financial value.

Nothing typifies this philistine attitude more than the activities of the conquistadores in the New World in the 15th century; many of the items they plundered from the Aztec and Inca empires were of extraordinary beauty, but this did not interest the Spaniards in the slightest. Everything made of precious metal was melted down and converted to bankable bullion and spendable coin. With the coming of the Renaissance, however, art and learning were appreciated for their own sake, and it became

fashionable for cultured princes to surround themselves with works of art. The very fact that works of art were appreciated for their own sake, however, gave them a financial value; as soon as demand goes up, so does the price. In the late 18th and early 19th centuries there was a positive mania for collecting forgotten art treasures from across the world, which, it was felt, had been undiscovered and unprotected for too long.

In 1803 Britain's Lord Elgin loaded the famous Elgin Marbles onto a boat and packed them off to his Scottish castle. The marbles were the frieze of the Parthenon in Athens, and Elgin's motives were not entirely selfish, for the Parthenon had suffered terribly under years of Turkish rule, and its treasures were in danger of being completely ruined. Elgin simply felt that Britain was a safer place for them than Greece. Unfortunately, the sight of his workmen attacking the ancient ruins with hammer and chisel was thought to be too much, and Elgin received little but criticism for his pains. He eventually tried to sell his collection to the British Museum for £74,240 ($300,000), a sum he calculated would scarcely cover his expenses. He was forced to settle, in the end, for £35,000 ($140,000) and a good deal of disillusion. The Elgin Marbles are still the subject of a sometimes bitter ownership dispute between Britain and Greece.

Napoleonic plunder
And yet, Elgin's actions were as nothing compared to one of his contemporaries. Napoleon Bonaparte was, quite shamelessly,

Far right:
The motives of art thieves vary. Many, of course, are just in it for the money, but others steal paintings to publicize themselves or their particular aims. This picture, Vermeer's 'Girl with a Guitar', was stolen in 1974 to support the cause of the IRA. Despite threats that it would be destroyed on St Patrick's night, it was returned largely undamaged.

Above:
Some paintings seem to attract the attention of art thieves. Rembrandt's portrait of Jacob de Gheyn III is one of the world's most stolen pictures. It was stolen from a London gallery in 1966, 1973 and 1981: each time it was recovered. In 1983, however, it was stolen again, and has never been seen since.

one of the greatest looters of art treasures in history. Unlike most of his predecessors, he was not in it for financial gain, either personally or nationally – he was in it for the cultural glory of France. He believed that France was rightly the artistic center of the world and, by virtue of her political strength, she was doubly entitled to house and protect all the great treasures of Europe. With extraordinary arrogance he proclaimed, 'All men of genius are French, no matter in what country they happen to have been born.' To that end, he appointed an aristocratic political survivor, a man of great energy and discerning taste, Baron Dominique Vivant Denon, to be in charge of his campaign.

Denon shared Bonaparte's ideals and lack of qualms. He began his work in Egypt, taking not only treasures but invaluable information from the tombs of the Pharaohs, sometimes working under fire as the French troops overran the country. With Napoleon's successful campaign in Italy, the opportunities available to him were extraordinary. He even took the huge statues of the Horses of San Marco from outside the basilica in Venice in December 1797. The people of Venice were so outraged that they rioted in the streets, and French troops had to keep them back at bayonet point. But away the horses went, to be paraded in triumph around the Champs de Mars in Paris with other examples of cultural booty. The Louvre – originally called the Musée Napoleon – was given to Denon to house the outstanding collection. Napoleon's regime did not last

forever, however, and when it collapsed the European allies soon arrived to collect their lost property. To the disgust of Denon and outrage of many of his colleagues, over 2,000 paintings and hundreds of sculptures, engravings, and *objets d'art* were repatriated, including the Horses of San Marco.

Hitler's hauls

A century later, Adolf Hitler had precisely the same idea. A skilled, if unimaginative, painter and architect himself, Hitler dreamed of fulfilling his frustrated artistic leanings by creating a collection that would remain a permanent testimony to the achievement of his Reich. He had grown up in the town of Linz, in Austria, and had fond memories of it, so he made Linz the object of his obsession. He planned to have the whole town rebuilt in the heavy, approved Nazi style, arranged around a hugh showpiece gallery. 'Sonderauftrag Linz' (Special Operation Linz) set out to glean works of art from every country Nazi Germany overran – with the possible exception of Russia, whose ancient artistic tradition Hitler despised on racial grounds.

In conquered countries art treasures were simply confiscated. In allied countries, a modicum of decorum was observed. Many of Italy's art treasures had been taken to the mountaintop refuge of Monte Cassino monastery; when fighting threatened the monastery, the German soldiers offered to evacuate the treasures to a safe place. Most were taken under guard to the Vatican, but a few were mislaid on the journey and found their way to Germany. Vichy France undertook to look after Belgium's priceless Van Eyck altarpiece from Ghent Cathedral, but the Germans traced it and took it away anyway. Treasures belonging to murdered Jews were taken over by the state, and many a minor Nazi official, seeking to curry favor, acquired a picture or a statue and presented it to the Fuehrer. At the end of the war, thousands of objects intended for Linz were found in an Austrian saltmine. And Hitler's chief lieutenant, Hermann Goering, a man of more flamboyant tastes and keener appreciation than Hitler, went into business on his own account, amassing a superb collection of paintings and sculptures at his Karinhall villa. With the fall of the Nazis in 1945, the Allies were faced with the tremendous headache of trying to return such works of art to their rightful owners. The work is still going on today. Many items were lost or mislaid simply because of the anarchic state of Europe in the aftermath of hostilities. The Hungarian Crown of St Stephen, for example, a medieval crown with great symbolic significance, was stolen by Hungarian fascists to prevent its falling into the hands of the

Left:
Adolf Hitler, along with Napoleon, was one of the great looters of European history; both men intended to collect the world's art treasures to the glory of their empires. Hitler's lieutenant, Hermann Goering, indulged in the business on his own account, however; this is part of his private treasure collection, discovered by the Allies at the end of World War II.

Below:
Shortly before the fighting began at the abbey of Monte Cassino, the Germans evacuated the monks. The monastery's priceless collection of art treasures was packed up and removed 'for safe keeping', although several items disappeared en route, and have never been seen again.

advancing Russians. It was handed over to the Americans for safe keeping, and kept in Fort Knox for many years, until President Carter had it returned to the Hungarian people in 1978.

A catalog of crimes

Most art thieves lack the extraordinary resources of a Hitler or a Napoleon. And yet they, too, have their curious motives. The most famous art theft of them all, Vincenzo Perugia's 1911 attempt on the 'Mona Lisa' was prompted by a desire to restore a great work to his native Italy, a belated compensation for the ravages of Napoleon. In 1939 Serge-Claus Bogousslavsky stole Watteau's 'L'Indifférent' from the Louvre because, he said, he loved Watteau and that particular painting had been badly treated and needed loving restoration. A jury decided Bogousslavsky's high ideals had, in fact, damaged the painting, and sent him down for four years. In 1958 two small Van Dycks, then worth about $14,000, disappeared from a gallery in Aix-en-Provence in France. Three days later they were found on a window ledge with a note explaining that they had been taken as a bet. In 1974 Vermeer's 'Girl with a Guitar' was stolen from Britain's Kenwood House by Irish nationalists, who demanded that the sisters Dolours and Marion Price, in prison on the mainland for terrorist crimes, should be returned to their native Northern Ireland. Despite threats that the picture would be burned on St Patrick's night, it was eventually abandoned in a London churchyard.

A popular theory is that behind many art crimes is an eccentric collector, keen to own his favorite paintings whatever the cost, locking them away in a secret vault where only he may see them. Such a scenario is by no means impossible – remember Goering – and there are persistent rumors of two such characters, one a

US newspaper baron, the other a South American beef millionaire. In 1983 a Greek olive oil manufacturer was arrested and charged with having commissioned thefts from a Budapest museum, but the charges were dropped. In December 1983 one of the world's largest art thefts occurred at Mexico's National Anthropology Museum. The robbers took 140 priceless gold, jade, and obsidian artifacts, including some of the famous Mayan artifacts from the well at Chichén Itzá. Since the trade in pre-Columbian treasures has a shady element to it, it is possible that these items might have ended up in private collections. Certainly they were all too well known to be sold publicly. Similarly, the paintings stolen from the Marmottan Museum in Paris can have value only for ransom or to a collector.

By far the most usual motive for art theft is the hope of a quick profit. Many small treasures are stolen from private collections and can be sold to unsuspecting dealers. In the case of the more valuable pieces, their fame counts against them, for they are often too hot to sell. As the gang which robbed several wealthy galleries on the French Riviera in the 1960s discovered, the only hope is usually to ransom them back to the owners, often at a fraction of the value.

And yet, art crime seems to be growing. Interpol, who try to keep a central record of stolen works of art, have up to 70,000 cases on their books at any one time. Some works seem to suffer more than others. Rembrandt's portrait of Jacob de Gheyn III has the distinction of being one of the world's most stolen masterpieces. It was taken from London's Dulwich Picture Gallery in 1966, recovered, stolen again in 1973, and again in 1981. Finally, thieves broke in through a skylight and took it away once more in 1983. It has yet to be found.

Theft of the Mona Lisa

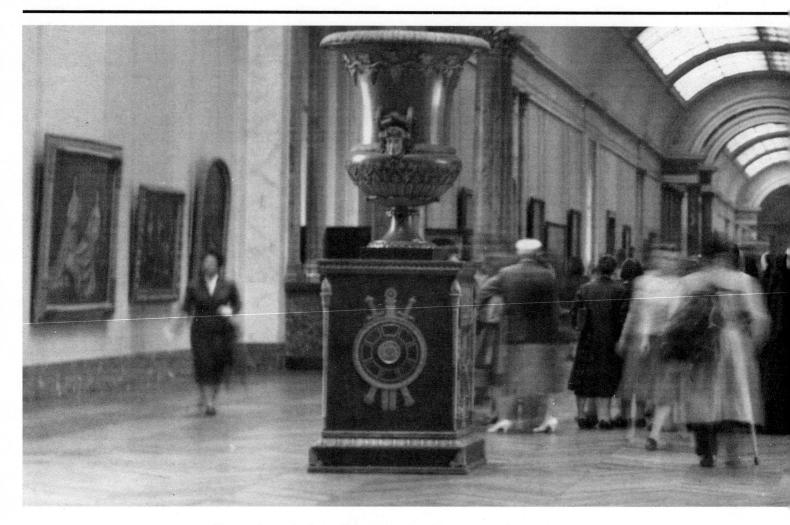

The smile on the lips of Leonardo da Vinci's famous portrait of the 'Mona Lisa' is justifiably renowned, and many have wondered as to its significance. On at least one occasion, this most famous of artistic ladies had cause to look mysterious for, as a Paris paper commented at the time, she had eloped, and it had caused quite a stir.

Leonardo painted his masterpiece in Florence between 1503 and 1506, his subject Mona Lisa, second wife of Zanobi del Giocondo — sometimes called 'La Gioconda'. It was clearly a picture he valued himself, for when Leonardo emigrated to France he took it with him. It was eventually sold to Francis I for 4,000 gold coins. It hung in the royal palaces of Fontainebleau or Versailles, and may have adorned Napoleon's bedroom at the Tuileries. In 1804 it was presented to the Louvre gallery in Paris.

One day in 1911, a maintenance man noticed that the 'Mona Lisa' was missing from her usual place on the wall. He joked to his colleagues that it had been removed to prevent his stealing it, but they did not suspect anything wrong. The painting was frequently removed to be photographed, copied, or engraved. The next morning, Brigadier Poupardin of the Louvre guards also noticed that it was missing, but thought that it had been taken for photographing. About 9 in the morning, a painter, Louis Beroud, who was completing a picture of the gallery which housed the masterpiece, asked where it was. He was told that the photographer was copying it. When it had not been returned by midday, he insisted that Brigadier Poupardin investigate. The red-faced guard commander returned with the breathtaking news that the picture was nowhere to be found.

The world reacts

When the news reached the press that afternoon, it was greeted with incredulity. One paper ran the story under the simple headline *Inimaginable!* To the Parisian public, deeply in love with their national art treasures, it was a monstrous crime. Many simply refused to believe it. It was all a hoax, they said, to prove the painting's vulnerability, to embarrass some official, or to sell the newspapers. The prefect of police was called in, and began a systematic search of the Louvre. When it had first been opened in 1793, France's foremost gallery had contained a mere 155 objects, but now it covered 49 acres, housed over 500,000 items, and contained a maze of underground storage chambers. The magazine *L'Illustration* offered a reward of 40,000 francs for the return of the painting, no questions asked: *Paris-Journal* topped it with an offer of 50,000 francs. The police managed to piece together the crime.

The thief had probably hidden in the building overnight and, before too many guards were about, had simply unhooked the picture from the wall. He'd gone into a store-room, stripped the binding from the back of the frame, and taken the picture out, leaving the frame behind. He'd unscrewed a bolt to get through one door, and then bumped into a plumber in the corridor. The plumber assumed that the thief was a fellow workman who was lost, and showed him out of the building.

For several months, Paris was in uproar. Everyone had theories about the crime. Some thought that the painting had been stolen by an art student in love with the face; others that it had been destroyed by a lunatic. Psychics pronounced on its fate. Mysterious strangers were questioned, rumors abounded. So did recriminations – the Louvre's curator, Theophile Homolle, was sacked, and security at the gallery tightened.

Above:
The gallery in the Paris Louvre where the 'Mona Lisa' hangs. The relaxed attitude of the guard is suggestive of a casual attitude to security, and it is certainly true that Vincenzo Perugio walked off with the painting with comparative ease.

Below:
One of the greatest artists of the twentieth century, Pablo Picasso, pictured with his wife in 1919, several years after the 'Mona Lisa' affair. Picasso's friend, the avant-garde poet Apollinaire, became involved in the 'Mona Lisa' scandal because he had been offered other stolen artifacts from the gallery. Both men were questioned over the Leonardo theft, but were completely innocent.

Far right:
Probably the most famous painting in the world, Leonardo da Vinci's 'Mona Lisa'; but its fame did not save it from the indignation of abduction in 1911. The motives of the thief still arouse speculation, and it has been suggested that, during its absence from the Louvre, the painting was copied, and the copies sold off as the original to several unscrupulous American collectors.

There was an interesting diversion involving the poet Guillaume Apollinaire and his friend Pablo Picasso. Some years earlier, it transpired, Apollinaire had been offered two statues stolen from the Louvre by an eccentric named Géry Pieret. He had refused them, but Picasso had bought them. In the aftermath of the Mona Lisa robbery Pieret confessed to another statue theft, and Picasso and Apollinaire, in panic, tried to return the first two to a newspaper. Apollinaire was arrested and grilled about the theft of the 'Mona Lisa' itself. Happily, he was innocent, and the police reluctantly released him.

The finding

It was two years before the masterpiece turned up. One day in November 1913 an Italian art dealer, Alfredo Geri, received a note from Paris offering him the 'Mona Lisa'. At first he was inclined to treat it as a joke, but on second thoughts he showed it to his friend Giovanni Poggi, the curator of the Uffizi gallery. They decided to arrange a meeting with the letter-writer. He turned out to be a tall, thin young man named Vincenzo Perugia. Perugia led them back to his lodgings, took a parcel out from under his bed, and unwrapped the missing masterpiece.

The finding of the 'Mona Lisa' caused almost as much of a sensation as its theft. In the Italian Chamber of Deputies a fist fight between political rivals broke up when the news was announced. Perugia, pressed for a motive, declared he had stolen it (by posing as a workman to enter the Louvre) to redress Napoleon's looting of Italian art – although cynics pointed out that Perugia had asked Geri for 500,000 lire for its return. He was tried, found guilty, and sentenced to one year and 15 days' imprisonment, although, on appeal, he was released after seven months. The painting itself went on a tour of Italy, where it drew rapturous crowds, particularly in Florence, before being returned to the embarrassed officials in France.

It is impossible to estimate the value of such a painting. It was not, and never would be, for sale. However, the *New York Times* wryly pointed out that if Francis I had bought it for 400 gold pieces in 1506, that was equivalent to about $9,200. At 3 percent compound interest alone, by 1913 it would have been worth $1,629,528,062. And interest on that sum would run up at the rate of $94.30 a minute...

The strange case of the disappearing Duke

Above:
Experts study the Goya masterpiece after its return to the Gallery in May 1965. The Duke was lucky; there was some minor damage but basically the picture was in good condition. Not all works of art are treated with such consideration when stolen.

Far right:
In Goya's rich portrait, Britain's greatest general, the Duke of Wellington, has a slightly indignant look, as well he might. In 1961 the Iron Duke was stolen from London's National Gallery, and remained missing for several years while the thief unsuccessfully tried to ransom it back for charity.

On 21st August 1961, London's National Gallery in Trafalgar Square had an averagely busy day – some 5,690 visitors passed through its doors. One, at least, left in a highly unorthodox fashion, climbing out through a back bathroom window. With him he took Goya's portrait of 'The Duke of Wellington'.

Initial police investigations drew a blank, but 10 days later the news agency Reuters received an anonymous note, written in plain capitals and bearing a London postmark. After carefully describing notes and stretching devices on the back of the frame, which only the thief would know, it went on to say, 'The picture is not, and will not be for sale – it is for ransom – £140,000, to be given to charity. If a fund is started, it should be quickly made up, and on the promise of a free pardon for the culprits, the picture will be handed back… All good people are urged to give, and help the affair to a speedy conclusion.' Ransom demands for stolen works of art are no rarity, but seldom has one claimed such a Robin Hood motive – stealing from the rich to give to the poor! If the note was intended to attract publicity, it certainly succeeded. The influential London *Times,* intrigued, ran a piece which likened the thief to the fictional gentleman cracksman Raffles, who was famed for his ability to steal the unstealable. Perhaps, suggested *The Times,* the thief might like to test his skill by returning the picture to a major Goya exhibition without being caught? The thief was not tempted, and a large reward offered by the gallery had no more luck.

More offers

As time went by, the missing Goya became a *cause célèbre,* the intrigue surrounding it being expressed by no less a person than the movies secret agent James Bond. When tackling the dastardly *Dr No,* Bond was surprised to see the missing Goya on the archvillain's wall. For all the success there was in tracing it, it might well have been there.

In July 1962, Reuters received a second letter. 'The Duke is safe,' it maintained. His temperature cared for, his future uncertain. Once again it demanded a ransom for charity, and once again it was refused. In December 1963 there was a third letter, suggesting that the major newspaper proprietors should pay a small tax on every 1,000 copies sold. Finally, in March 1965, the thief, clearly becoming frustrated, issued his 'fifth and final demand'. He offered to return the picture if it were put on display for several weeks, and the attendance fees given to charity. 'Liberty was risked in what I mistakenly thought was a magnificent gesture,' it ended sourly, 'all to no purpose so far.' Perhaps gambling on the assumption that such a literate and conscientious crook was unlikely to cause the painting lasting damage, the authorities still refused to comply.

In May 1965, a tall, nervous young man, who gave his name as Mr Bloxham, left a package at the left-luggage counter of Birmingham railroad station. Seventeen days later the newspaper the *Daily Mirror* received an anonymous note which included a left-luggage ticket. When police went to collect the parcel, they found the missing Goya, deprived of its frame but otherwise in good condition.

Belated confession

And there the curious tale might have ended, had the culprit not suddenly given himself up. Kempton Bunton, an unemployed truck driver from Newcastle upon Tyne, walked into Scotland Yard and confessed to having stolen the Goya. He described how he had entered the gallery up a ladder left near a back window by workmen. He had no particular need for the Goya – despite the fact that it had been acquired by the gallery only a few weeks before for $392,000. Any famous painting would have done. There were no guards around, so he took the picture and left the way he had come in. Asked why he was confessing to the crime, he said that he felt sure someone was about to inform on him to claim the reward. He seemed confident that the police would not be able to prove criminal intent, and without that he would not be convicted.

The trial began in November 1965 and lasted for 12 days. Bunton claimed that his motive had been to protest on behalf of old-age pensioners who, like everyone else in Britain, are required to pay a license fee for the use of a television set. He was able to produce evidence of a history of protest in this cause. True enough, the prosecution were unable to prove criminal intent, and Bunton was acquitted on the charge of stealing the Goya. He was unable to account satisfactorily for the frame, however, and was sentenced to three months for the theft of that. And thus the mystery of the missing Duke was finally wrapped up.

Riviera follies

Above:
Bonnard's vivid study of the harbor of St Tropez. The clear, fresh light of the Riviera attracted first the artists, then the beautiful people, and finally the thieves who preyed on both. This picture was among a haul of no less than 57 paintings stolen from the Museum of the Annunciation (Annunciade) in St Tropez in 1961.

In 1892 the painter Paul Signac's boat was forced into the small harbor of St Tropez by a sudden squall. He immediately fell in love with the bay's sandy beaches and blue sea and skies, and St Tropez soon became a favorite haunt of France's bohemian community. Gradually it attracted the rich and famous from all over the world, until the Riviera and St Tropez in particular became the world's most famous playground for beautiful people with time on their hands. And in the 1960s it was the scene of a spectacular series of art thefts which might have come straight from a glossy heist movie.

The first robberies to excite attention occurred at Villefranche and Menton. A wealthy Paris dealer Armound Drouant, had a villa at Villefranche which housed some of his private collection. On the night of 11th January 1960, it was broken into and 30 paintings removed. The police had not solved this crime before the museum at Menton was robbed two months later of seven paintings, including a Modigliani. A week later the Colombe d'Or at Saint-Paul-de-Vence was turned over.

The Colombe d'Or was an inn opened by Paul Roux in the 1920s. It was a great favorite among visiting artists who, if they couldn't pay their bills, found Roux accommodating enough to settle for a picture instead. In this way Roux built up a superb collection of early 20th-century paintings. When Roux died in 1955, his son took over the business and operated in the same way, undaunted by the fact that the value of his uninsured collection was mounting year by year. Then, on the night of 23rd March 1960, thieves broke into the Colombe d'Or and stripped it of 20 paintings valued at the time at $600,000, including several Braques, a Picasso, and works by Matisse and Modigliani.

The Riviera police, embarrassed by three crimes in a matter of months, were in a frenzy. In a manner worthy of Inspector Clouseau, they rounded up various suspects, interrogated them, and were forced to release them as innocent. On one occasion a suspect was followed by gendarmes disguised as nuns. The

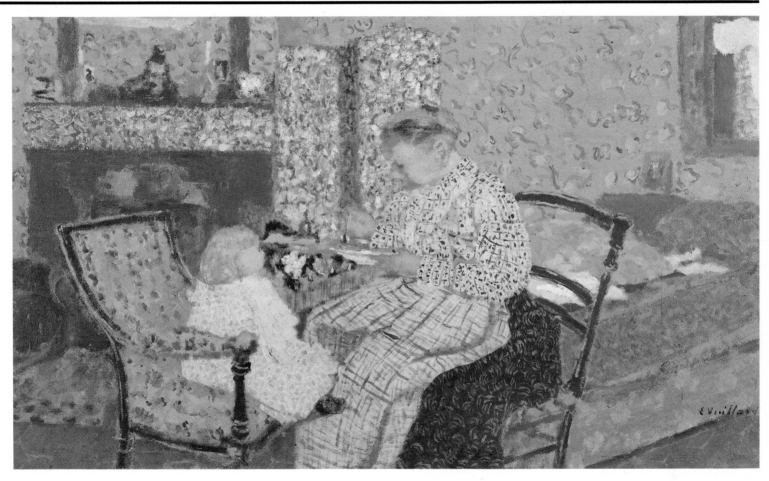

thieves clearly did not intend their haul to be sold to shady dealers, for Roux received several ransom demands. The police kept secret the details of any negotiations, but on 14th February they received a phone call from someone claiming to be a priest who suggested that they went to the baggage department at Marseilles station. They were handed a large parcel which contained 19 of Roux's paintings. While excited observers were still wondering whether Roux had paid a ransom – rumored to be $20,000 – another, even more spectacular robbery took place.

In 1955 a millionaire, Georges Grammont, died, leaving his collection of more than 100 Impressionist paintings and other objets d'art to St Tropez, with provision for a disused chapel to be set up as a gallery. Named the Museum of the Annunciation, it became the finest gallery on the Riviera, Dunoyer de Segonzac, the town's most respected resident painter, being appointed curator. On 15th July 1961 thieves used a key to enter via an outside gate, broke open an inside door, and carefully selected 57 of the collection's most important pieces, including two of Segonzac's own works. A tramp sleeping on a park bench nearby reported that he heard a Citroën drive off in the early hours, and a local resident complained about noisy revelers, but it was not until the arrival of the cleaning lady the next morning that the crime was discovered.

Segonzac was deeply upset, the museum authorities were appalled when they realized that the paintings were not insured against theft, and the police were beside themselves with frustration. Three weeks later the thieves struck again.

The raid at Aix

The town of Aix-en-Provence was having an exhibition devoted to the works of its most famous son, Paul Cézanne. It had been arranged by a Cézanne expert, Professor Novotny of Vienna, and included works loaned by the Louvre and individuals and institutions in

Above:
Vuillard's tender 1907 painting of a mother and child was one of the paintings stolen in an extraordinary and spectacular theft which had more than a touch of farce about it, since the French Police adopted bizarre disguises during the case, and the thieves could not get rid of the loot. In the end, however, all the paintings were recovered.

America. In the light of the Riviera crimes, the Aix officials insisted on tight security. The grounds were patrolled by armed guards, and searchlights lit up the outside at night. But it was all to no avail. Some time between 1 and 4 in the morning on Sunday, 13th August, several men climbed a wall from a neighboring schoolyard and dropped down into the gallery's garden. They landed on a scattering of ripe mulberries fallen from an overhanging tree, and the juice stained their shoes, leaving a trail of purple footprints to mark their progress. They cut a wire which they assumed was connected to an alarm system (it wasn't, the gallery didn't have one) then one or two of them scaled the wall and entered through an open third-floor window. There was a guard in the building, but his room was on the first floor, and he heard nothing. A lady curator who lived on the third floor slept through the whole crime. The thieves took six Cézannes from the first room, abandoning a large portrait of the artist's father, which was too securely fastened to the wall, and then went up a further floor, taking two smaller pictures. All eight paintings, including 'The Artist's Sister' and one of the famous 'Card Players' series, were passed out and lowered from the window. They made a clean getaway and, once again, it was not until the next morning that the pictures were missed.

With more than 60 pictures now missing, the French Minister of Cultural Affairs, André Malraux, intervened personally, exhorting the police to recover the pictures intact no matter what the cost. It was assumed that the same gang was responsible – said to be eight men operating from Marseilles – because the *modus operandi* was essentially the same. Both the St Tropez and Aix thefts were committed on public holiday weekends – the first on Bastille Day, the other on the Feast of the Assumption. There were the usual rumors: the crimes were a hoax; they had been carried out by an eccentric collector; they were committed by various sinister strangers. Two American art students were arrested carrying pictures at a railroad station, and it was several hours before the police were convinced the works belonged to the students.

By now, Segonzac had received the first ransom note for the St Tropez collection. The thieves demanded 50 million francs against a threat that the pictures would be destroyed. To prove that they were serious the thieves sent a small piece cut from one of Segonzac's own watercolors. With each demand they sent a further piece. Segonzac frantically tried to raise the money from among his friends and admirers.

Picking up the pieces

The Cézanne paintings from Aix had been insured, however, and negotiations proceeded apace. From the insurers the thieves demanded 25 million francs. The police refused permission for the ransom to be paid, but in April 1962 they received a phone call directing them to a car abandoned in a Marseilles side-street. For several hours the police watched the car, hoping to trap whoever had left it there, but had no luck. When they finally checked it they found the eight Cézannes on the back seat, minus their frames. The pictures had to run one more risk however, before being safely returned because the car taking them away broke down and burst into flames. Fortunately this proved to be no more destructive than had the criminals. It was widely rumored that a ransom had been paid.

Meanwhile, poor Segonzac was still negotiating for the return of the Annunciation collection. Far too well known to risk selling to a collector, and unable to blackmail an insurance company, the thieves were reduced to trying to raise what cash they could with guarantees of immunity from police prosecution. Segonzac

Left:
An impressionistic study of London's Westminster, one of the pictures stolen from the Annunciade. Art theft has much to recommend it to the criminal, great values being placed on single, easily moveable items, but its overriding drawback is that the fame which gives the pictures value also make them too hot to handle. The Riviera robberies are the classic example of this principle.

offered to exchange one of his own pictures as part of the ransom, but his offer was not accepted. This was, perhaps, surprising, since whoever organized the crime was clearly interested in Segonzac.

In November 1962, the usual anonymous phone call told the police to look in a rundown barn outside the village of Villiers-Saint-George, 50 miles from Paris. Villiers-Saint-George was one of Segonzac's early haunts, and he painted several views of it. The paintings were found rolled up hidden under heaps of straw. Some were slightly damaged by this rough treatment, but not seriously. Only one painting was still missing – the mutilated Segonzac watercolor.

The discovery of the paintings caused almost as much sensation as the robbery. Press and public demanded to know the details of behind-the-scenes maneuvering. Had a ransom been paid? A curiously precise figure of $68,000 was mentioned. To what extent had André Malraux intervened? Had there been a deal? Would the crooks be prosecuted? Inevitably, the police issued bland assurances; the important fact was, after all, that the paintings had been recovered.

The St Louis bonus

But the strange story of the Riviera capers has one final twist. Gradually, the authorities began to return the pictures to their rightful owners, and the insurers who had already paid out for the Cézannes untangled the legal complications and reclaimed their money. 'The Artist's Sister' went back to the St Louis Art Museum in America. Before it was put back on display the museum's conservator embarked on a program of cleaning and restoring. While doing so, he noticed that the back of the canvas was coated with thick layers of glue apparently concealing paint. He slowly and carefully stripped them off, and found a portrait of an old peasant woman underneath – an early Cézanne the artist had abandoned before reusing the other side of the canvas. The museum had bought 'The Artist's Sister' for $7,500 in 1934; by the time they got it back from the Marseilles gang, rising prices and the second portrait had increased its value to $225,000!

The Marmottan theft

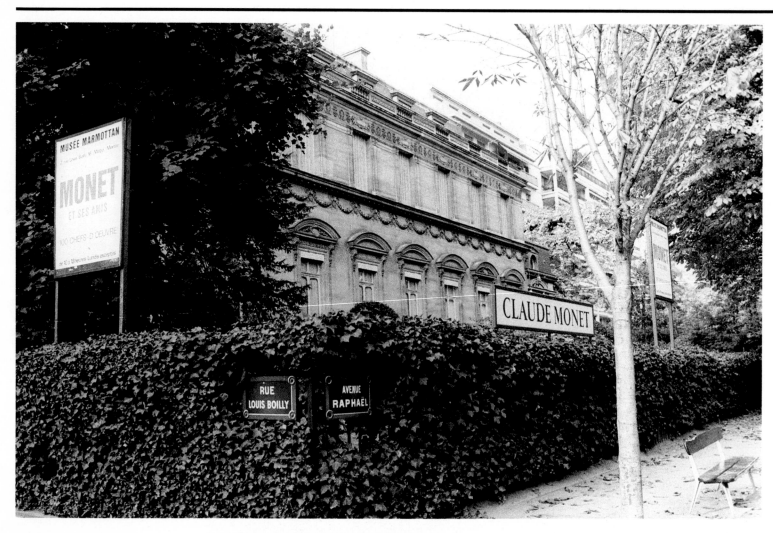

Above:
The Marmottan Museum in Paris, once the home of wealthy collector Paul Marmottan, and now a gallery specializing in Impressionist works, particularly those of Monet. On Sunday, 27th October, 1985, thieves robbed the gallery at gunpoint, and stole nine priceless paintings.

There were perhaps 30 foreign tourists in the Musée Marmottan on the morning of Sunday, 27th October 1985. An elegant town house near the Bois de Boulogne in Paris, the museum had once been the home of Paul Marmottan, an art historian and collector. It housed one of the best collections of Impressionist paintings in France – over 50 by Claude Monet alone, with others by Renoir and Morisot, as well as furniture and treasures from the First Empire period. This priceless collection was protected by an expensive alarm system, connected to a local police station. It was, however, switched off during opening hours, since visitors had been known to trigger it accidentally.

At about 10 in the morning, five men double-parked their car outside the museum, calmly walked in through the main entrance, and carried out one of the most sensational crimes in recent art history. Two of them produced guns and held up the tourists and attendants. The others studiously selected the paintings they wanted. Five Monets, two Renoirs, a Berthe Morisot and a Narusé were stolen, the Monets from the first floor, the others from rooms on the second floor. A glass case was deliberately and carefully smashed open and the contents removed. 'They knew the layout of the museum perfectly, and knew exactly what they wanted,' said an attendant. The thieves were in the building for little more than five minutes, and left through the front door, carrying the paintings with them. The pictures were put in the trunk, and the car drove off with the trunk open. In its planning and execution, the crime was breathtakingly simple. By the time the police were called, the car was long gone. To the time of writing, nothing more has been heard of the pictures.

Left:
'Portrait of Poly, Fisherman of Belle-Isle', one of three works by Claude Monet stolen in the Marmottan robbery. This picture has an estimated value of $300,000, although Monet's work is too well known to have much black-market value.

Above:
Monet's 'Camille Monet and Her
Cousin at the Beach, Trouville',
worth perhaps $1,100,000.
Among the thieves' haul was
'Impression Sunrise' by the same
artist, undoubtedly the first and
possibly the most famous work
from the Impressionist school. Its
value has been nominally set at
$15,000,000, but it is difficult to
see how thieves could ever sell
such a picture.

The first Impressionist painting

The theft was particularly stunning because it
included the most famous Impressionist
painting of them all – Monet's 'Impression
Soleil Levant' ('Impression Sunrise'). A study of
the waterfront at Le Havre, this rippling tableau
of misty blues and oranges was first exhibited at
the salon of the photographer Nadar in 1874.
Painted in a much more expressive style than
was the fashion of the day, it created such a stir
in the art world that one critic was prompted to
say, 'Impression – I thought so . . . half-finished
wallpaper is more finished than this sea-piece.'
It was a comment which coined the term
'Impressionism', and gave birth to the name of a
movement which was to prove the most
innovative and influential in modern art history.
'Impression Soleil Lèvant' is, therefore, rightly
regarded as the first Impressionist painting.

Because this painting is so famous, it is
impossible accurately to estimate its value,
although the museum's curator, the painter
Yves Brayer, estimated shortly after the theft
that it was 'at least 100 million francs'
($13 million). This is regarded as a conservative
estimate; others have put it as high as
$14 million. Nor were the other paintings
financial lightweights – the Morisot had an
estimated value of $1 million; the other Monets
varied between $175,000 and $280,000, and
Narusé's portrait of Monet some $50,000.

The extreme fame of the pictures does not
necessarily augur well for the thieves, however.
As usual with the theft of a particularly well-
known painting, it would be impossible to sell
on the black market, simply because it would be
too 'hot'. And in this case, the museum did not
have its treasures insured – so the alternative
method of cashing in on the crime, by holding
the pictures to ransom, is unlikely to
succeed.

Yet the thieves knew exactly which pictures
they wanted, and were working to a plan which,
though simple, was so thorough that it hardly
seems likely that they would not have made
some plans for the disposal of the paintings.
Since they've made no demands public, it
seems improbable that they were motivated by
politics or a desire for notoriety.

Perhaps this is one of those few cases where a
wealthy, eccentric, and unprincipled collector
might be said to be behind it all, commissioning
the theft of his favorite paintings for his
exclusive appreciation.

Left:
'Young Lady at a Ball' by Berthe Morisot, the first woman to join the Impressionist movement. The breathtaking audacity of the daylight robbery, and the historical and artistic value of the pictures stolen, make it one of the greatest art crimes ever.

Appendices

This cannon is part of the wreckage of the French frigate *L'Hermenie*, which went down off Bermuda in 1883. The islands of the Caribbean are a treasure-hunter's paradise, offering unrivaled opportunities for underwater exploration.

Appendix I

Treasure-hunting for all

Few people have the resources and opportunity to track down a lost treasure such as the *Nuestra Señora de Atocha* or the good fortune to stumble accidentally upon one like the Mildenhall silver. But diligent searching can reveal many old or not-so-old objects with both aesthetic appeal and sometimes surprising value, and there is always a chance that, in seeking them, a true lost treasure may come to light. The hunt can add excitement to such mundane activities as clearing an attic or cellar, or even going to a garage sale.

By and large, we shall ignore the higher realms of antique-collecting and fine art – expensive fields requiring considerable knowledge and experience, and full of pitfalls for the unwary – and concentrate instead on items that could lurk in the lumber-room or be revealed in a weekend's amateur excavation.

Coins, tokens and badges
Coins are the treasure-hunter's quarry *par excellence.* They are durable, may possess both intrinsic and rarity value, and have a habit of being lost or forgotten. They have also been collectors' items for centuries, which carries two advantages: old collections often lie forgotten in dusty niches, possibly gaining considerably in value as they do so; and they are well cataloged, making it easy for anyone to check the significance of a find.

Any gold or silver coin is worth the intrinsic value of its precious metal content multiplied by its rarity value and, usually, its condition. High on the list according to all three categories is the uncirculated US Brasher doubloon of 1787,

which would probably fetch $1 million or more on the market today. It is of gold, only about half a dozen examples are known and, because it was not circulated, its condition is excellent. Copper, bronze, and cupro-nickel coins have little intrinsic value, but their rarity may command a high price. One example each is known of the British George VI half-crown of 1952 and the Elizabeth II penny of 1954, and the latter fetched some $30,000 when it was sold in 1978.

Tokens, issued in many countries by shops, taverns, and other establishments when small coin was scarce, are of base metal and usually low value, perhaps up to $100 in some cases. A curio among these items is a 19th-century replica of a Georgian British 'spade guinea' (itself a valuable coin), intended as a gambling chip. Badges range from military insignia to the emblems of medieval pilgrims and medals. Depending on the precious metal content and rarity, some individual medals can be worth up to $75,000.

Stamps and notes
Stamps, bank notes, and related items such as stock certificates share many of the qualities of coins, although without intrinsic value or durability. Again, they have been collectors' items for a long time, so forgotten collections come to light relatively frequently; stamps also appear, of course, among hoards of letters or postcards. Probably the most famous rare stamp is the British Guiana 1c magenta of 1856, which is worth around $1 million, but there are others, such as the 5c US Blue Alexandria of 1846,

Far right:
A vast collection of 17th-century pewterware has been recovered from the old pirates' base of Port Royal, near Kingston in Jamaica, now largely submerged beneath the Caribbean. Pewter is not intrinsically valuable, but these artifacts are priceless to archaeologists and historians for what they reveal of everyday life in the past.

worth as much or more. Misprinted sets of stamps are often valuable.

Ceramics and glass

Pottery remains are the most common items found in the excavation of both prehistoric and historic sites all around the world. Usually they occur as broken fragments or potsherds, but occasionally whole or slightly damaged objects are preserved. In most cases, they are of little monetary value; however, they are of enormous worth to archaeologists in establishing dates, cultural evolution, and trade patterns, so they should under no circumstances be treated lightly when seeking more appealing material.

Fine china and glass are a different story, and well-preserved early or rare examples can be worth a fortune. A single Meissen piece by J J Kaendler, the 18th-century modeler, may fetch $250,000. Chinese Ming porcelain found in quantity in an 18th-century shipwreck was provisionally valued at 'millions of dollars' in 1986; one Ming vase reached $600,000 at auction in 1974. A single Roman glass cup fetched more than $700,000 at auction in 1979.

Roman glasses are not too likely to turn up outside museums and collections, but porcelain may well do so. Objects our great-grandparents bought for a few dollars have increased enormously in value over the past few years, in some cases by as much as 18 times their 1960s price. Of course, they must be genuine; pottery makers' marks are easy to forge reasonably convincingly. Worcester, Doulton, Derby, and Spode are some names to look for in 19th- and early 20th-century pottery and porcelain; in the 20th century, Wedgwood's 'Fairyland lustre' ware has become extremely valuable. In glass, 19th-century items from Boston & Sandwich and Mount Washington in the US, and from Nailsea in Britain, are now collectors' items.

A growing area of interest among collectors of limited means is 19th-century bottles and transfer-printed ceramic pots and jars. The bottles come in a whole range of exotic colors and shapes, while post-1840 pots may have colorfully printed lids and sides. Such items can often be found in pre-1900 garbage tips, and hunting them can be a cheap and rewarding way of learning some basic excavation techniques (*see* Appendix III). Most of these bottles and pots are probably only worth up to about $30 each, but some rare examples can fetch $4,000 to $5,000.

Weaponry

Primitive weaponry, such as stone or copper arrowheads and spearheads, is relatively common and not usually of high value. Collecting it was particularly fashionable among antiquaries of the 18th and 19th centuries, along with associated relics such as Indian war-bonnets, and ready-made collections are frequently found. Deposits of primitive weapons unearthed when excavating a site should be left undisturbed and reported to a museum or professional archaeologist.

Daggers, swords, and firearms can vary enormously in value, but in very general terms those worth most date from the 16th to the end of the 18th century, when lavish decoration with precious or semi-precious stones and gold or silver was almost compulsory among the well-to-do. At the top end of the scale, sale prices can go to $200,000 or more. Handguns and rifles of the 19th and early 20th centuries are increasingly sought by collectors, and so are some later models such as the World War II German Luger.

Furniture
Louis XIV, Sheraton, Chippendale, and Hepplewhite are some of the magic names, but few of us are likely to stumble across them unawares, at least in the original; innumerable imitations are still being churned out. There is a growing market, however, for what might be called functional or country-style furniture, and that frequently comes to light, often camouflaged with layers of paint, in lumber-rooms and barns. One of the most sought-after categories is the solid, plain Shaker style of the 18th and 19th centuries. Another is the British Arts and Crafts Movement, although later examples were sometimes mass-produced. Pre-1914 'furniture with a purpose', such as the washstand, is increasingly valuable. A rarity in this category is the Virginia stool-shower with built-in back-scrubber of 1830.

By contrast, examples of early 20th-century Art Nouveau are now being eagerly hunted. Single chairs from recognized masters of the form can be worth $120,000.

Small items
In addition to the categories already mentioned, there are many other small items that have become recognized targets for collectors, and therefore have a value well in excess of their original cost. Where they do not fall into an established class of antiques ('antique' usually denotes something dating from the 5th century AD to the turn of the present century; items after that period are often termed 'bygones'), they are sometimes called 'collectables'.

One of the widest ranges of small collectables can be labeled for convenience 'tools of the trade'. It embraces everything from early scientific instruments, such as astrolabes, microscopes, and telescopes, to bobbins and thimbles. Kitchen equipment is a popular sub-category, including corkscrews, various types of molds, and such rarities as American sorghum

skimmers. Old fountainpens, inkwells, and blotters are also sought after.

Other functional items that many people collect include musical instruments, door furniture, coat-hooks and stands, umbrellas, walking canes, pipes, cigarette cases, tobacco jars, purses, visiting-card holders... the list is virtually endless. Among nonfunctional objects to look out for are musical boxes, board games and pieces, toy soldiers and vehicles and dolls and dolls' houses.

Assessing the finds
The first question most people ask upon finding a treasure is 'What's it worth?', even if they have no intention of selling. There are several sources to turn to for help.

One of the best, if the item seems particularly valuable, is an established auction-house. Most of the major companies now offer a no-strings advisory service, including the price to expect at auction. Consult them on gold and silverware, jewelry, porcelain, fine art, and furniture, and perhaps on coins, stamps, and medals, old books, maps, and documents. With less valuable items in any of those categories, or collectables, auction-houses tend to prefer to deal with collections that can be sold as one lot.

Specialist dealers can also give an opinion. However, their valuation amounts effectively to the price they are prepared to pay, and does not take account of their profit margins.

Museums and archaeological societies can provide advice and assistance on the age and authenticity of an object, but are unlikely to commit themselves on the value, unless they themselves wish to acquire the find.

There are many books on antiques and other collectors' items. They can help in identifying a find, but it is often quite difficult to relate the object to a two-dimensional picture or a written description. Use them for a preliminary check and then seek personal advice if the object appears valuable. Some catalogs – such as those for stamps and coins – include estimates of value. Those can be misleading and disappointing unless the accompanying notes are read carefully, as so much depends on condition. The literature on collectable bygones is sparser than that for recognized classes of antiques. In many cases, though, there are collectors' clubs and magazines to turn to for help.

Far left:
Old guns are precious collector's items, though few match this monster for scale. Cast in bronze, it was recovered from the wreck of the 17th-century Swedish warship *Kronan* off the island of Oland in the chilly waters of the Baltic. Altogether, 15 cannon were found initially, out of a total of 128 the *Kronan* carried.

Below:
Minted in Peru and Mexico, these Spanish coins date from the early 18th century and were retrieved from the wreck of the galleon *La Holandesa* off the coast of Florida.

Appendix II

Law and the treasure-hunter

The laws governing treasure-hunting vary in their details around the world, but one basic principle holds true almost everywhere: other than on his own freehold property, the treasure-hunter does not have any automatic right to pursue his quest (on leased or rented land, permission should be obtained in writing from the landlord – see below); even on his own property he may not be automatically entitled to keep his finds. The same applies to treasure-hunting in territorial waters. The position of wrecks in the open seas is more complicated, and has been the subject of lengthy lawsuits in the United States and Europe. However, several parties may have an overriding claim to a deep sea wreck – the navy of the country to which it belonged, the insurers, if they have met claims arising from it, the successors of the owners, and even salvagers who previously took the wreck in tow, but lost it.

So before setting out on a treasure-hunt, check the national or local laws carefully, and the procedures for reporting finds. Some countries insist that all items recovered must be reported to the police or to the national archaeological service, and that national museums have the first claim on them, with or without full compensation for the finder. Many impose restrictions on the export of antiquities.

Permission to explore a site should be obtained in advance, and is essential on privately owned or leased land. It should be in writing, and contain an agreement with the landowner on the division of any valuable items found, as well as on the mechanics of the exploration – such things as means of access,

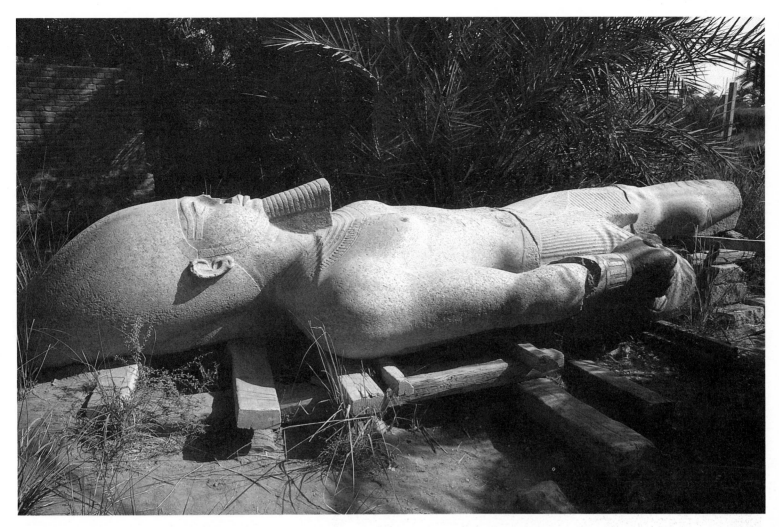

restoration of the site, and the time-limit. The rules applicable to public land are more variable, but always with the proviso that the treasure-hunter has no automatic right to explore them. Parks, commons, and village greens generally come under the aegis of the local council. Open land is generally administered by the state. River banks, river and lake beds, and foreshores may be privately owned or, if not, be the nominal property of a public authority. In America and Europe, restrictions are increasingly being placed on their exploration, even if they are public places. A permit is now required to excavate material from the foreshore of the River Thames in London, for example. The use of metal-detectors may be subject to licensing and other restraints (*see* Appendix III).

In Anglo-Saxon law, the concept of 'treasure trove' often creates confusion. It applies to objects deliberately hidden by a previous owner with the apparent intention of returning to claim them later. By implication, the hiding-place must, by its character, have some degree of permanence. Thus, a hole in the ground or a cavity in a house-wall might be used to conceal treasure trove, but coins found in the pocket of

antique clothing in an attic would probably not be classed in that category. In England, only articles containing gold or silver can be treasure trove; in Scotland and elsewhere, the definition is much wider. The decision as to whether a particular find is treasure trove or not is taken by a coroner or equivalent public official. The finder may receive the monetary value, or get the objects back if they are not wanted by a museum.

In addition to the legal requirements governing access to sites and the notification of finds, there are a few commonsense rules responsible treasure-hunters should observe. Archaeological sites and ancient monuments should be left completely alone unless you are working with a recognized archaeological group. If you chance upon an archaeological site, report it to the local museum, and notify it of any unusual historical finds. Leave the site clean and tidy, filling in any holes before you go. Do not damage crops or frighten animals.

Finally, beware of lethal objects such as unexploded ammunition, bombs, or mines, and containers that may hold dangerous materials. Mark the spot, and report them immediately to the police.

Above:
This remarkable statue of a Pharaoh is at Memphis, a ruined ancient city (14 miles south of Cairo, Egypt).

Far left:
Many ancient sites were ruthlessly ransacked for their artifacts by so-called antiquarians up until the end of the 19th century, and in some places the process is still going on. Knossos, the capital of the Bronze Age Minoan civilization on Crete, benefited from the sensitive excavation techniques of Sir Arthur Evans (1851-1941), who spent 30 years laying its secrets bare.

Appendix III

Equipment and its uses

Right:
A diver uses a metal detector to examine the site of the main anchor of a Dutch East Indiaman wrecked off the coast of China in the early 18th century. This is a relatively advanced and expensive piece of equipment, but cheaper versions are widely available.

Far right:
Inexpensive metal detectors have helped to make treasure-hunting a hobby for many people. There are several different types, all of which can be mastered with a little practice. But in many parts of the world, there are laws governing both their technical specifications and where they may be used. It is always advisable to check these.

The high-tech paraphernalia of professional treasure-hunters, particularly those working underwater, is expensive. You can assemble a basic kit for use on land quite cheaply, and probably already own many of the items needed. Some of them can be used underwater, too, but in addition you will need a diver's knife, a strong 'finds bag' and underwater writing materials and torch, as well as, of course, scuba-diving equipment if you intend to work for any length of time. No one should use scuba equipment without proper instruction beforehand; unaccompanied diving is dangerous. Before you dive, pay careful attention to the conditions – surface weather and winds, tides, currents and wave heights, water temperature, and underwater visibility.

Probably the most important item in your kit is a trowel – not the rounded gardening type, but the kite-shaped kind with a pointed blade, used by bricklayers. In the hands of an experienced excavator, such a trowel is a precision instrument capable of removing delicate items from the ground without damage, and prising the top layers of dirt from them. Some people prefer a flat-bladed screwdriver for the same purpose. Underwater, the diver's knife can be used, with care. In very wet ground, a small hand-fork is sometimes better.

If the objects you are seeking lie fairly deep, remove the top layers of soil with an ordinary spade, or a fork if you are working on a garbage site. But make sure you switch to the trowel as you get lower down, so as not to damage any precious material. The depth of large objects, such as a chest or the foundations of a building, can be assessed beforehand by using a probe. An ordinary thin metal rod at least 2 feet (60cm) long makes a suitable probe, but specialty stores sell more intricate versions with T-shaped handles and threaded points. Some also have a device for bringing up soil samples.

A hand-sieve is needed to sift soil or sand for small objects, such as coins, that might otherwise be missed. If you use only one, it should have a medium-coarse mesh. Professional archaeologists generally use several in succession, with progressively finer meshes, to trace, for example, gems that have become separated from their mountings.

Polythene bags are essential for packing and removing small objects, and it is useful to have a haversack or some other large bag for carrying the equipment and the finds. For serious treasure-hunters, a map of the area, a compass, and a notebook for recording details of locations and objects are important, too. It is often useful to take a large ball of twine and pegs, to mark out the area being searched and to avoid covering the same ground twice by accident.

A further aid, for picking up small items of

ferrous metals, is a powerful magnet. Marine magnets enable you to explore shallow water without getting wet.

Metal-detectors

The arrival on the market of relatively cheap and efficient metal-detectors has stimulated many more people to take up treasure-hunting as a hobby. Unfortunately, their indiscriminate and irresponsible use has excited the wrath of archaeologists, landowners, and conservationists, particularly in Europe. To some extent, this is being overcome by the formation of metal-detecting clubs that work closely with archaeologists and other experts to ensure that potentially important sites are not damaged or pillaged. In many countries, such as Britain, a license is needed to use a metal-detector, and there are legal restrictions governing the frequencies on which they operate. In the US, there are controls on the detector's electrical power output.

There are three types of detector, and all have their devotees, though none is capable of registering a large coin at depths of much more than a foot. The pulse induction (PI) detector is relatively insensitive to thin materials — an advantage if the object is merely a scrap of silver paper — and to the mild conduction effects occurring in wet soil or sand, which can be misleading to the operator. On the other hand, PIs tend to pick up ferrous metals, quite often worthless, at considerable depths, and cannot be satisfactorily tuned to distinguish between ferrous and non-ferrous metals. Induction balance (IB) and beat frequency oscillator (BFO) machines can be adjusted to make the distinction (at least, the more expensive versions can), or to reject the cupro-nickel used in modern 'silver' coins. They can also be tuned to filter out ground effects, and some IBs come with immediate reset buttons to adjust them for changes in the natural conductivity of the soil.

Eager digging that reveals only a drinks can is an all-too-familiar experience for detector operators. It is an inevitable incident when using PI machines, and may happen with the other types even if they are set to distinguish between ferrous and non-ferrous metals (most cans are predominantly tinplate over steel). Ring-pulls and can tops are aluminum, thus registering as non-ferrous. The machine has not been made that can tell the difference between a ring-pull and a gold ring of similar proportions.

However, after some practice with a detector, the operator learns from its responses to judge the size and shape of underground objects, and also the variations in response that may be due to minor temperature fluctuations.

Cleaning the finds

The cleaning and restoring of ancient objects is a precise craft. In general, all you should do is remove as much of the soil as you safely can by gentle brushing; a soft toothbrush is useful in the final stages. After that, seek expert advice from a local museum, antique shop, or jeweler. Items made entirely of gold can be washed in warm, soapy water, but that treatment can damage other materials if, for example, the gold is part of a necklace. Marine encrustation on any valuable object should normally be removed by an expert. Organic materials, such as wood, leather, or textiles, found in water or waterlogged soil should be kept immersed in water from the site in a polythene bag or suitable container until cleaning by an expert can begin.

Far left:
Divers working on an ancient wreck in the Mediterranean are accompanied by a diving-bell. Artifacts can be raised to the bell and stored there temporarily, enabling the divers to stay underwater for longer. They can also preserve their oxygen supply by occasionally breathing the air in the bell.

Below:
Off Kyrenia, on the coast of Cyprus, a diver uses an air saw to help him in excavating a wreck. Professional archaeologists can use such saws safely, but in amateur hands they can cause untold damage to valuable remains.

The removal of accumulated sand and silt is a major problem for underwater excavators, but over the past 40 years a number of devices have been developed to cope with it. Here, an air pump shifts sand from the remains of *De Liefde* in the Shetland Isles.

F10153C Multimedia Lost Treasures MW128 8.7.86
1st proof 1st setting
Drive B   10153C.MUL
CFD 5

Picture Credits